MORE AUSTRALIAN LEGENDARY TALES

Collected by

Mrs K.Langloh Parker

Drawings by Tommy McRae

ETT IMPRINT

Exile Bay

This edition published by ETT Imprint, Exile Bay 2023.

First published in 1898 by Melville, Mullen & Slade, Melbourne.

ETT Imprint
PO Box R1906
Royal Exchange NSW 1225
Australia

Design by Tom Thompson

Cover: Original cover art by Tommy McRae.

ISBN 978-1-923024-23-6 (pbk)
ISBN 978-1-923024-24-3 (ebk)

CONTENTS

Preface 5

THE CRANE AND THE CROW 12

BEEREEUN THE MIRAGE MAKER 13

BOHRAH THE KANGAROO AND DINEWAN THE EMU 21

GHEEGER GHEEGER, THE COLD WEST WIND 23

BILBER AND MAYRAH 26

BRÄLGAH THE DANCING BIRD 28

HOW THE SUN WAS MADE 34

STURT'S DESERT PEA, THE BLOOD FLOWER 36

PIGGIEBILLAH THE PORCUPINE 42

GAYARDAREE THE PLATYPUS 44

HOW MUNGGHEE, or MUSSELS, WERE BROUGHT TO
        THE CREEKS 47

WURRUNNAH'S TRIP TO THE SEA 50

WALLOOBAHL THE BARK LIZARD 55

GOOLAYYAHLEE THE PELICAN 57

MUNGOONGARLEE THE IGUANA AND
        OUYOUBOOLOOEY THE BLACK SNAKE 60

WAYAMBEH THE TURTLE AND WOGGOON
        THE TURKEY 65

WHERE THE FROST COMES FROM 69

BUBBURR THE GIANT BROWN AND YELLOW SNAKE 71

THE YOUAYAH MAYAMAH, OR STONE FROGS 74

A LEGEND OF THE FLOWERS 78

THE FROG HERALDS OF THE FLOOD 82

EERIN, THE SMALL GREY OWL 84

THE LEGEND OF NAR-OONG-OWIE,
        THE SACRED ISLAND 88

Glossary 92

Dedication

TO

THE EUAHLAYI-SPEAKING PEOPLE
IN GRATEFUL RECOGNITION OF
THEIR EVER-WILLING ASSISTANCE
IN MY FOLK-LORE QUEST

PREFACE

I must begin the preface to a new series of Australian Legendary Tales by thanking the press and public for the, to the collector, gratifying reception they gave the first one. There are many persons who have individually expressed their interest in my work so kindly that I would like to name them here and publicly thank them, but some of them are of such world-wide fame that to do so might seem a mere self-advertisement at their expense. Should this come under their notice, they will, I hope, understand my reticence, and accept my gratitude.

The present series of legends have all been collected by myself from the Blacks, as were the previous ones. But in this instance I had much help given to me by friends, who either told or sent me scraps of legends they themselves had seen or heard. On receiving any such I immediately made inquiries amongst the Blacks, and I was often enabled to complete the scraps, gaining through their hints a whole legend. For should the local tribes know nothing of what I wanted to hear, I would get them to make inquiries of wandering Blacks from other tribes whom they might meet during their periodic "walk-abouts," or at corroborees they attended. I myself have had opportunities of knowing well members, of nine tribes, though that which I know best is the Euahlayi-speaking one, of which the Noongahburrahs are a branch.

As far as I know, only one of the legends in this series has previously been printed entire. This is one of my own collecting from a Wiradjari black fellow, "The Crane and the Crow," and appeared in the Sydney *Bulletin*.

Some of the Blacks who have helped to build up this series belong to the Murrumbidgee, Darling, Barwon, Paroo, Warrego, Narran, Culgoa and Castlereagh rivers; the Braidwood, Yass, Narrabri, and other districts of New South Wales; to the Balonne, Maranoa, Condamine, Barcoo, Mulligan rivers, and the Gulf country in Queensland. But I have confined myself as far as possible to the Noongahburrah names, thinking it would create confusion if I used those of each dialect—several different names, for example, for one bird or beast. To such as were told in song I have tried to retain something of the rhythmical rendering. I have no doubt a skilled writer could have mosaicked these legendary scraps with flowery language into a beautiful work of art, but I have preferred to let the Blacks as far as possible tell their legends in their own way, only adding such explanations as seemed necessary to make them clear to the English reader.

I trust the fact that these legends belong to a stone age, an age when everything was rough hewn, will not be lost sight of by readers. Ever since I have been collecting folk-lore I have endeavoured to keep as many of the "coloured people" about me as I could in various capacities, even going the length that "Uncle Remus's" creator did, namely, of "at times sacrificing digestion to sentiment," the practical result of which has been that many scraps of folklore were revealed to me of which, but for this daily intercourse, I should probably never have heard. For instance, a young Bootha brought in the lamp one evening; seeing some big grey moths fluttering round it she said: "No good, Comebeegeeboon darngliealdah, no tomahawks here; you'll get burnt for nothing." Then I learnt that the spirits send these grey moths as soon as it is dark to the camps to steal tomahawks for them. The bag-like back of their bodies is supposed to be the comebee (bag) they carry these in if they get them, but most often they are dazzled by the light of the fires, and blindly flutter into them, getting singed as they do round the lamp.

While walking through the bush after heavy rain, I came across some very brilliant fungi, growing on to dead trees. I picked off a piece, and on my return, going out to speak to some of the Blacks, I carried this fungus in my hand. A little black child, seeing its bright colour, came towards me as if to get it, but his mother quickly interposed, saying in an alarmed tone: "Don't let him touch it. It is way-way. Don't let him touch it." Then she told me that all fungi growing on trees were the bread of ghosts, and if a child touched any he would be spirited away by the ghosts. She said these fungi were luminous at night so that the ghosts could see them.

Walking through the bush, as I often do, with some of the Blacks, I hear many little scraps. Quite lately, while going along the edge of one of the plains we put up some spur-winged plover, who went off harshly screeching. I asked why the bird had that strange spur. Because, they said, a long time ago, a black fellow called Bahldurrahdurrah, as the plovers are now, had been noted for never going abroad without poison-tipped spears, from which even a scratch was fatal. When he died he was turned into a plover, and has his spears still, in the modified form of the spurs on the wings; he brings these forward if he wishes to injure anything, holding it between them, with fatal result.

On similar occasions I learnt that when the sun, as it sometimes does in summer, goes down like a fiery red ball, it is the reflection of wattle gum on it that makes it so bright. After such a sunset, if they go out for gum, they are certain to find quantities; they say. The gum they melt in water, making it into a half liquid jelly which they eat with relish, and which they say has great strengthening properties. That when the moon looks very yellow after it has risen on a winter's evening, it is a sign of frost. "The Meamei have told Bahloo they will send frost to-night. He is going to keep himself warm; look at his bright fire," they say.

When they see a tree that usually grows on the plains on the ridges, or vice versâ, they say: "There are two who have married wrongly; that Coolabah must have run away from her tribe with a Bibbil. And now the wirreenuns, or wizards, have turned them into trees."

I often come in contact with instances of their deeply ingrained superstitions. One morning a very fine healthy specimen of a young native woman was scrubbing the verandahs. As I passed her, she said, "I might die soon, Innerah." (They call me Innerah in the sense of boss-woman.) On inquiry I found some young man whom she had declined to marry had stolen a lock of her hair, and was now making his way with it to the wirreenuns of the Boogahroo. Should he reach them and they agree to burn it, she would die. There was some hope for her, she said; her totem clan, the Beewees, were very strong out that way, and, having been warned, might intercept him. Should he succeed in causing her death, so long as any of her tribe were alive they would be at enmity with his, and the feud would go on from generation to generation.

Another day a girl came to borrow a horse to go down the river to see her sister, whose baby, a messenger had just come to tell her, was dead. She went, and on her return I asked if the baby were buried. She told me the wirreenuns had put its breath back in it and it was alive again. On my doubting that it had been really dead, she brought two or three witnesses to corroborate her story, and they described how the two wirreenuns had caught the breath just after it left the body, put it back through the child's mouth, and then set to work to suck the sickness out of the body, with the result that the baby recovered.

It was in the summer of 1896, when the six weeks of a heat wave caused so many deaths in this district from heat apoplexy, that the Blacks first saw Marmbeyah, the ghost with the green boondee, about here. The next summer I said one day to a black woman that I hoped we should not hear of so many deaths that season. "Oh no," she said, "there won't be any this year because a black fellow has killed Marmbeyah, who caused the deaths by knocking the people on the back of their necks with his green boondee." The black fellow is supposed to have seen this evil-dealing ghost in front of him one day, he himself being unobserved, when he stole up and flattened him with his boondee, thus saving his people and the whites from further sickness of the heat apoplexy kind. We have in the camp an old woman who is supposed to call up spirits—and they do come. She gave us a test of her power one day, which I am bound to say compared favourably with any séances of a like nature I had seen before, inasmuch as she held hers in the light of day. She never drinks hot tea nor any sort of liquid which would heat her internally; did she do so she says the spirits would be driven out and she be powerless as a medium of communication with them; it is, she says, because the black people drink the "grog" of the white people they are losing their ancient power; in the past they never drank any hot liquid.

It was the same old woman who accurately foretold the breaking up of a drought. The oldest woman of this tribe having died, was buried the next day. The Blacks told me I could go to the funeral, and on the way the old spiritualist walked beside me. Seeing the droughty desolation of the country, I asked her when she thought it would rain again. Coming very close to me, she half whispered, "In three days I think it; old Beemunny tell me when she dying that s'posing she can send 'im rain, she sent 'im three day, where her yowee go long a Oobi Oobi." Beemunny died on Wednesday night, and we went to bed on Saturday with the skies as cloudless as they had been for weeks; in the middle of the night we were awakened by the patter of raindrops on the iron roof. All night it rained and all the next day.

Since my first series came out I have heard some items which more fitly complete four of the legends in it, which completions I now add. To "Mullyangah the Morning Star" might be added that under the tree in which Mullyan's gahreemay or camp was, the spring of water which was there then is still so, and from time to time it throws up various sorts of mammoth and strange bones belonging to a past age, which the Blacks say are the remains of Mullyan's many victims, whose bones were dropped from the tree into this spring, called Guddee, which is in the Brewarrina district.

To "The Galah and Oolah the Lizard," some Blacks add that the present colouring of the bird, grey and rose-pink, is owing to her having rolled in the dust as the blood streamed down both sides of her head from the wound the bubberah, thrown by Oolah, had made, staining for ever her breast and underpart of her wings, the dust toning the blood-red down to rose-pink.

It is to the legend of "Mooregoo the Mopoke, and Bahloo the Moon," that we owe a black fellow's reason for a halo round the moon. Ever since the storm in that legend when Bahloo built himself a dardurr, he has done so before rain. Seeing a halo the Blacks say, "Bahloo has built his dardurr, there will be rain."

To "Deereeree the Wagtail and the Rainbow" they add that Bibbee, who made the Euloowirree or rainbow, put snakes at its end to guard it, and if any one goes near it, these savage flat-headed snakes will kill them.

The former series were all such legends as are told to the black piccaninnies; among the present are some they would not be allowed to hear, touching as they do on sacred subjects, taboo to the young.

The Legend of Nar-oong-owie, the Sacred Island, was not heard directly by myself from the Blacks, but was first told to me, when a child, by my grandmother, and was sent recently to me by my uncle in much the same form, having been told to him by a full-blooded aboriginal of Southern South Australia.

To the legend of "Dinewan the Emu, and Whan the Crows," some natives add that when Dinewan's wives (the crows) threw the hot coals over him his wings were burnt off, and that singed appearance which has been theirs ever since given to the feathers where the stumps of the wings are.

K. Langloh Parker
Bangatre, Narrea River, New South Wales
September 1898

MORE AUSTRALIAN LEGENDARY TALES

COLLECTED·BY·K·LANGLOH·PARKER

THE CRANE AND THE CROW

The crane was a great fisherman. He used to hunt out the fish, with his feet, from underneath the logs in the creek, and so catch numbers.

One day when he had a great many on the bank of the creek, a crow, who was white at that time, came up. He asked the crane to give him some fish.

"Wait a while," said the crane, "until they are cooked."

But the crow was hungry and impatient, and would not cease bothering the crane, who kept saying, "Wait. Wait."

Presently the crane turned his back. The crow sneaked up and was just going to steal a fish. The crane turned round, saw him, seized a fish, and hit the crow right across the eyes with it. The crow felt blinded for a few minutes. He fell on the burnt black grass round the fire, and rolled over and over in his pain. When he got up to go away his eyes were white, and the rest of him black, as crows have been ever since.

The crow was determined to pay out the crane for having given him white eyes and a black skin.

So he watched his chance, and one day when he saw the crane fast asleep, he crept quietly up to him holding a fish-bone. This he stuck right across the root of the crane's tongue.

Then he went off as quietly as he had come; careful, for once, to make no noise.

The crane woke up at last, and when he opened his mouth to yawn he felt like choking. He tried to get the obstruction out of his throat. In the effort he made a queer scraping noise, which was all he could give utterance to. The bone stuck fast.

And to this day the only noise a crane can make is, "gah-rah-gah, gah-rah-gah!" This noise gives the name by which he is known to the blacks.

BEEREEUN THE MIRAGE MAKER

Beereeun the lizard wanted to marry Bullai Bullai the green parrot sisters. But they did not want to marry him. They liked Weedah the mocking-bird better. Their mother said they must marry Beereeun, for she had pledged them to him at their births, and Beereeun was a great wirreenun and would harm them if they did not keep her pledge.

When Weedah came back from hunting they told him what their mother had said, how they had been pledged to Beereeun, who now claimed them.

"To-morrow," said Weedah, "old Beereeun goes to meet a tribe coming from the Springs country. While he is away we will go towards the Big River, and burn the track behind us. I will go out as if to hunt as usual in the morning. I will hide myself in the thick Gidya scrub. You two must follow later and meet me there. We will then cross the big plain where the grass is now thick and dry. Bring with you a firestick; we will throw it back into the plain, then no one can follow our tracks. On we will go to the Big River; there I have a friend who has a goombeelgah, or canoe, then shall we be safe from pursuit, for he will put us over the river. And we can travel on and on even to the country of the short-armed people if so we choose."

The next morning ere Gougourgahgah had ceased his laughter, Weedah had started.

Some hours later, in the Gidya scrub, the Bullai Bullai sisters joined him.

Having crossed the big plain they threw back a firestick, where the grass was thick and dry. The fire sped quickly through it, crackling and throwing up tongues of flame.

Through another scrub went the three, then across another plain, through another scrub and on to a plain again.

The day was hot; Yhi the sun was high in the sky. They became thirsty, but saw no water, and had brought none in their haste.

"We want water," the Bullai Bullai cried.

"Why did you not bring some?" said Weedah.

"We thought you had plenty, or would travel as the creeks run, or at least know of a goolahgool, or water-holding tree."

"We shall soon reach water. Look even now ahead, there is water."

The Bullai Bullai looked eagerly towards where he pointed, and there in truth, on the far side of the plain, they saw a sheet of water. They quickened their steps, but the further they went, the further off seemed the water, but on they went ever hoping to reach it. Across the plain they went, only to find on the other side a belt of timber, the water had gone.

The weary girls would have lain down, but Weedah said that they would surely reach water on the other side of the wood. Again they struggled on through the scrub to another plain.

"There it is! I told you so! There is the water."

And looking ahead they again saw a sheet of water.

Again their hopes were raised, and though the sun beat fiercely on them they marched, only to be again disappointed.

"Let us go back," they said. "This is the country of evil spirits. We see water, and when we come where we have seen it there is but dry earth. Let us go back."

"Back to Beereeun, who would kill you?"

"Better to die from the blow of a boondee in your own country than of thirst in a land of devils. We will go back."

"Not so. Not with a boondee would he kill you, but with a gooweera, or poison stick. Slow would be your deaths, and you would be always in pain until your shadow was wasted away. But why talk of returning? Did we not set fire to the big plain? Could you cross that? Waste not your breaths, but follow me. See, there again is water!"

But the Bullai Bullai had lost hope. No longer would they even look up, though time after time Weedah called out, "Water ahead of us! Water ahead of us!" only to again, and again, disappoint them.

At last the Bullai Bullai became so angry with him that they seized him and beat him. But even as they beat him he cried all the time,

"Water is there! Water is there!" Then he implored them to let him go, and he would drag up the roots from some water-trees and drain the water from these for them.

"Yonder I see a coolabah; from its roots I can drain enough to quench your thirst. Or here beside us is a bingahwingul; full of water are its roots. Let me go; I will drain them for you."

But the Bullai Bullai had no faith in his promises, and they but beat him the harder until they were exhausted. When they ceased to beat him and let him go, Weedah went on a little way, then lay down, feeling bruised all over, and thankful that the night had come and the fierce sun no longer scorched them.

One Bullai Bullai said to her sister: "Could we not sing the song our Bargie used to sing, and make the rain fall?"

"Let us try if we can make a sound with our dry throats," said the other.

"We will sing to our cousin Dooloomai the Thunder; he will hear us, and break a rain cloud for us."

So they sat down, rocking their bodies to and fro, and, beating their knees, sang:

"Moogary, Moogaray, May May,
Eehu, Eehu, Doongairah."

Over and over again they sang these words as they had heard their Bargie, or grandmother, do. Then for themselves they added:

"Eehu oonah wambaneah Dooloomai
Bullul goonung inderh gingnee
Eehu oonah wambaneah Dooloomai."

Which meant:

"Give us rain, Thunder, our cousin,
Thirsting for water are we.
Give us rain, Thunder, our cousin."

As long as their poor parched throats could make a sound they sang this. Then they lay down to die, weary and hopeless. One said faintly: "The rain will be too late, but surely it is coming, for strong is the smell of the Gidya."

"Strong indeed," said the other. But even this sure sign to their tribe that rain is near roused them not; it would come, they thought, too late for them. But even then away in the north a thundercloud was gathering. It rolled across the sky quickly, pealing out thunder calls as it came to tell of its coming. It stopped right over the plain in front of the Bullai Bullai. One more peal of thunder, which opened the cloud, then splashing down came the first big drops of rain. Slowly and few they came until just at the last, when a quick, heavy shower fell, emptying the thundercloud, and filling the gilguy holes on the plain.

The cool splashing of the rain on their hot, tired limbs gave new life to the Bullai Bullai and Weedah. They all ran to the gilguy holes. Stooping their heads, they drank and quenched their thirst.

"I told you the water was here," said Weedah, "You see I was right."

"No water was here when you said so. If our cousin Dooloomai had not heard our song for his help we should have died, and you too."

And they were angry. But Weedah dug them some roots, and when they ate they forgot their anger. When their meal was over they lay down to sleep.

The next morning on they went again. That day they again saw across the plains the same strange semblance of water which had lured them on before. They knew not what it could be, only they knew that it was not water.

Just at dusk they came to the Big River. There they saw Goolayyahlee the pelican, with his canoe. Weedah asked him to put them over on to the other side. He said he would do so one at a time, as the canoe was small. First he said he would take Weedah, that he might get ready a camp of the long grass in the bend of the river. He took Weedah over. Then back he came and, fastening his canoe, he went up to the Bullai Bullai, who were sitting beside the remains of his old fire.

"Now," said Goolayyahlee, "you two will go with me to my

camp, which is down in that bend. Weedah cannot get over again. You shall live with me. I shall catch fish to feed you. I have some even now in my camp cooking. There, too, have I wirrees of honey, and durrie but ready for the baking. Weedah has nothing to give you but the grass nyunnoos he but now is making."

"Take us to Weedah," they said.

"Not so," said Goolayyahlee, and he stepped forward as if to seize them.

The Bullai Bullai stooped, filled their hands with the white ashes of the burnt-out fire, which they flung at him.

Handful after handful they threw at him, until he stood before them white, all but his hands, which he spread out and shook, thus freeing them from the cloud of ashes enveloping him and obscuring his sight.

Having thus checked him, the Bullai Bullai ran to the bank of the river, meaning to get the canoe and cross over to Weedah.

But in the canoe, to their horror, was Beereeun!— Beereeun, to escape whom they had sped across plain and through scrub.

Yet here he was, while between them and Weedah lay the wide river.

They had not known it, but Beereeun had been near them all the while. He it was who had made the mirage on each plain, thinking he would lure them on by this semblance of water until they perished of thirst. From that Dooloomai, their cousin, had saved them. But now the chance of Beereeun had come.

The Bullai Bullai looked across the wide river and saw the nyunnoos Weedah had made. They saw him running in and out of them as if he were playing a game, not thinking of them at all. Strange nyunnoos they were too having both ends open.

Seeing where they were looking, Beereeun said: "Weedah is womba, deaf. I stole his doowee while he slept and put in its place a mad spirit. He knows naught of you now. He cares naught for you. It is so with those who look too long at the Eer-dheer, or mirage. He will trouble me no more, nor you. Why look at him?"

But the Bullai Bullai could not take their eyes from Weedah, so strangely he went on, unceasingly running in at one end of the grass nyunnoos, through it and out of the other.

"He is womba," they said, but yet they could not understand it. They looked towards him and called to him, though he heeded them not.

"I will send him far from you," said Beereeun getting angry. He seized a spear, stood up in the canoe, and sent it swiftly through the air into Weedah, who gave a great cry, screamed "Water is there! Water is there!" and fell back dead.

"Take us over! Take us over!" cried the Bullai Bullai. "We must go to him, we might yet save him."

"He is all right. He is in the sky. He is not there," said Beereeun. "If you want him you must follow him to the sky. Look, you can see him there now." And he pointed to a star which the Bullai Bullai had never seen before.

"There he is, Womba."

Across to the grass nyunnoos the Bullai Bullai looked, but no Weedah was there. Then they sat down and wailed a death song, for they knew well they should see Weedah no more. They plastered their heads with white ashes and water; they tied on their bodies green twigs; then, cutting themselves till the blood ran, they lit some smoke branches and smoked themselves, as widows.

Beereeun spoke to Goolayyahlee the pelican, saying: "There is no brother of the dead man to marry these women. In this country they have no relation. You shall take one, and I the other. To-night when they sleep we will each seize one."

"That which you say shall be," said Goolayyahlee the pelican.

But the sisters heard what they said, though they gave no sign and mourned the dead Wedeah without ceasing. And with their death song they mingled a cry to all of their tribe who were dead to help them, and save them from these men who would seize them while they were still mourning, before they had swallowed the smoke-water, or their tribe had heard the voice of their dead. As the night wore on, the wailing of the women ceased.

The men thought that they were at length asleep, and crept up to their camp. But lo! it was empty! Gone were the Bullai Bullai!

The men heaped fuel on their fire to light up the darkness, but yet saw no sign of the Bullai Bullai.

They heard a sound, a sound of mocking laughter. They looked round, but saw nothing. Again they heard a sound of laughter. Whence came it? Again it echoed through the air.

It was from the sky. They looked up. It was the new star Womba, mocking them. Womba who once was Weedah, who laughed aloud to see that the Bullai Bullai had escaped their enemies, for even now they were stealing along the sky towards him, which the men on earth saw.

"We have lost them," said Goolayyahlee. "I shall camp alone," and he turned to go to his dardurr.

"They shall not escape me," said Beereeun. "I shall make a roadway to the skies and follow them. Thence shall I bring them back, or wreak my vengeance on them."

He went to the canoe where were his spears; having grasped them, he took too the spears of Goolayyahlee, which lay by the smouldering fire.

He chose a barbed one. With all his force he threw it up to the sky. The barb caught there, the spear hung down. Beereeun threw another which caught on to the first, and yet another, and so on, each catching the one before it, until he could touch the lowest from the earth. This he clutched hold of, and climbed up, up, up, until he reached the sky. Then he started in pursuit of the Bullai Bullai, and he is still pursuing them.

Since then the tribe of Beereeun have always been able to swarm up sheer heights. Since then too, his tribe, the little lizards of the plains, make, just like he did, the mirages to lure on thirsty travellers, only to send them mad before they die of thirst. Since then Goolayyahlee the pelican has been white, for ever did the ashes thrown by the Bullai Bullai cling to him, except where he had shaken them off from his hands, where are a few black feathers. The tribe of Bullai

Bullai are coloured like the green of the leaves the sisters strung on themselves, in which to mourn Weedah, with here and there a dash of whitish yellow and red, caused by the ashes and the blood of their mourning. And Womba the star, the mad star, still shines; Canopus we call it. And Weedah the mocking-bird still builds grass nyunnoos, open at both ends, in and out of which he runs, as if they were but his playground.

And the fire that Weedah and the Bullai Bullai made spread from one end of the country to the other, over ridges and across plains, burning the trees so that their trunks have been black ever since. Deenyi, the iron-barks, smouldered the longest of all, and their trunks were so seared that the seams are deeply marked in their thick black bark still, making them show out grimly distinct on the ridges, to remind the Daens of Beereeun the mirage maker for ever.

BOHRAH THE KANGAROO AND DINEWAN THE EMU

Bohrah the kangaroo lived in a grass nyunnoo with his wife Dinewan the emu. He was a great wirreenun.

One evening when Bohrah was lying down trying to sleep, Dinewan kept making holes in the roof of the nyunnoo.

"What are you doing that for?" asked Bohrah.

"Just for nothing," said Dinewan.

"Then get some grass and mend it up."

"There is no grass here."

"Then we will travel until we find some, for you won't let me sleep."

Off they went. It grew darker and darker every minute. Dinewan could not see where she was treading. She trod on bindeahs, which stuck into her feet and hurt her.

Limping along and feeling sore from the prickles, she said: "If you are such a great wirreenun as you say, surely you could make the dark roll away! Hunt it right away to another country. Let me see where to walk. My feet are very sore. If you could hunt the dark away, then you would be a great wirreenun. Oh my poor sore feet!" So crying she rubbed them against each other, which only made the bindeahs stick further in, raising rough lumps on her feet. Which lumps have been on the feet of her kind ever since, and their legs have been bare and hard up to the knee joint.

Now Bohrah the kangaroo was really a great wirreenun. While it was still quite dark he said: "We will sleep here, and I will hunt the dark away while we rest."

They laid down.

As soon as Bohrah was asleep, he sent his Mullee Mullee, or dream spirit, out from his body to gather up the darkness and roll it away to the westward. Having done so back came the Mullee Mullee to the body of Bohrah, who now woke up and saw what his spirit had done. He turned to Dinewan, whom he saw had slept with one eye and one ear open that she might see what he would do, and said:

"My Mullee Mullee has rolled the night from us. The darkness is no more. It is rolled away for ever from me. I and my people, from this out, shall be able to see to travel and feed at night as if it were day; for us there is no more darkness. You must feed in the daytime; I can as I please at night. You kept one eye and one ear open, you shall always sleep so. First one side of your head shall go to sleep and then the other, but never from henceforth both at once." And since that time so it has been even as Bohrah the kangaroo wirreenun said it should be.

GHEEGER GHEEGER
THE COLD WEST WIND

Durroon the night heron lived near a creek in which was an immense hollow log; this he used both as a fish and a man trap. He was by choice a bunna, or cannibal. The immense log was hollow and was under the water. In the middle of it Durroon had cut an opening.

When a Daen came to his camp Durroon used to ask him to go fishing with him, saying he wanted a mullayerh, or mate, as he was like a gundooee, one emu living alone. He wanted some one to go to one end of the log and drive the fish to the other, where he could catch them.

Seeing sense in this the Daen would agree, and off they would go, Durroon armed with his spear, to spear the fish when they came to his end of the log, so he said. But as soon as he had sent his mullayerh off to the far end, he would go along the log to the opening in the middle.

Unsuspecting treachery the Daen would come through the hollow log, driving the fish ahead of him. Directly he was under the opening Durroon would drive his spear swiftly into him, killing him on the spot. Then Durroon would drag his victim out, and, dismembering him, cook him.

In this way many men disappeared mysteriously until at length a clever crow wirreenun determined to solve the riddle of their disappearance.

Wahn the crow went to Durroon's camp. Durroon asked him to go fishing with him, but first offered him some good fat goodoo, or cod, he already had cooked.

Wahn agreed, and when they had finished their meal Durroon proposed they should go fishing, but Wahn said: "I ate too much goodoo. It was very fat. I ate a great deal and must have a sleep first before I start."

"All right. Plenty of time," said Durroon, feeling sure of his man-flesh supper.

Wahn went to sleep that he might send his Mullee Mullee, or dream spirit, to find out what was the trap Durroon had in the creek. The Mullee Mullee soon found out all about the opening in the top of the log, having done which back he came. Then Wahn, having learnt all, woke up, and said he was ready, so off they started. Durroon showed Wahn where to enter the hollow log, at the far end.

Now Wahn was a great wirreenun whom Durroon had no power to hurt, so he fearlessly went in. Durroon waited until he appeared under the opening, then down went the spear, evoking yells of "Wah! Wah! Wah!" from Wahn, who nevertheless went on and came out at the other end with the spear.

"What made you do that?" he said, pulling out the spear from where it had stuck in him.

"I did not mean to spear you," said Durroon. "I thought it was a big goodoo."

"Well, come on, I have had enough fishing," said Wahn. "You might make a mistake again."

On came Durroon, thinking Wahn really believed it was an accident, but no sooner had he caught up Wahn than he found himself speared in his turn, and fatally, as Wahn struck to slay.

About this time, Gheeger Gheeger the cold west wind had been blowing such hurricanes that the trees had been blown in all directions, and the crows' humpies scattered everywhere. "Now," thought Wahn, "I will catch Gheeger Gheeger and shut her up in this immense hollow log, but first I must dry the water off it."

This he set to work to do, and soon, one day when Gheeger Gheeger was tired out, after having blown down miles of trees, and cut the tribes with her cold blasts, Wahn sneaked upon her and drove her into the hollow log, which he blocked up at both ends and also at the hole in the middle.

Gheeger Gheeger roared and howled, but to no purpose.

"You only go about destroying things; you shall stay where you are," said Wahn.

Gheeger Gheeger promised to be more gentle in future if only he would let her out sometimes. For a long time Wahn would not trust her and kept her closely imprisoned, but after a while he let her come out occasionally, after she promised to blow no more gales. Sometimes she breaks her word and blows destructively as of old, but Wahn quickly captures her again, and hurries her back to her log prison.

There are holes now in this log and the breath of Gheeger Gheeger comes through, so unless Wahn finds a new prison for her, one day she will burst forth, and then there will be such a gale as never blew across the western plains before. Gheeger Gheeger will blast with her breath everything that stands in her way as she rushes to meet her loved Yarrageh, the spring wind which blows from the east Kumbooran, and which had of old been wont to meet Gheeger Gheeger as she blew from Dinjerrah the west, tempering, where they met, her cold with his own balmy warmth.

Twice a year the winds all met, holding great corroborees and wild revellings. Dourandowran came with his scorching breath from Gurburreh, the north, to meet his loved Gunyahmoo, the south-east wind which came from Bullimedeehmundi, to fan him with her softer, cooler breezes until his heat lessened, and he scorched those in his path no longer. Then from Nurroobooan, the south, blew Nooroonooroobin to meet Mundehwuddah, the north-west wind.

After the big corroboree the winds parted, each to return to his own country, hoping to meet again in another few months to again corroboree.

Hence the unrest of Gheeger Gheeger in the hollow log, and her much wailing that she could not break forth from her prison and rush to mingle her icy breath with the balmy one of Yarrageh.

BILBER AND MAYRAH

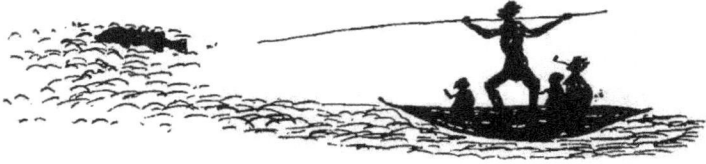

Bilber, the soft-furred sandhill rat, was once a man, and lived in a camp with Mayrah the wind for a mate. Mayrah was a strange mullayerh for a man, he was invisible. He could hold conversations with Bilber, but much as he desired it, Bilber could never see him. One day he said to Mayrah: "Why do you not become like me that I might see you?"

"I can see you," said Mayrah.

"Yes, I know that you can, but I cannot see you, only hear you. I know you are there because you eat the food before you. You catch opossums, and get honey, but though I go with you, following your voice, yet I can never see you, and I long to see some one again."

"But I can see you, so I am all right."

"But I cannot see you, and I long to see some one again. I must travel away somewhere and join others of my tribe. If I could only see you I would not wish for a better mullayerh."

"Well, I am off hunting now. Are you coming?"

"No, I will stay in the camp to-day."

Mayrah the wind went off, and when evening was at hand he was not yet back. Suddenly Bilber heard a roaring in the distance such as he had never heard before. Then he saw, where the sound seemed to be, a column of dust and leaves spouting up. "What sort of a storm is this?" he asked himself. "I never saw anything like it before. I will go up to that sand-ridge behind our camp and make a hole in the soft ground, into which I will get, so that this storm cannot take me away in its fury."

Off went Bilber hard as he could to the soft sandhill, the storm roaring behind him. There he made a hole and buried himself in it until the wind storm had passed.

Up came the wind, tearing on to the ridge, whirling round the camp, sending the bark and boughs flying about. On, on he went round Bilber's hole, but that he could not shift, so howling with impotent rage as he went, he passed on until his voice was heard only in the distance, and at length not at all.

After a time Bilber came out. He had been so safe and warm in his hole in the sand that he lived there ever afterwards, and there he took his wife, when he found one, to live. And to this day the Bilber tribe live in burrows in the sand. They still hear the voice of the old Bilber's mate, but never see his face, nor do they hear him speak any longer their language as of old, for so angry was he at Bilber's desire to see his face or leave him, that he only howls and roars as he rushes past their camps. And never since have any of the tribes seen where he camps, nor does any one know except the six winds that blow, and they tell the secret to none.

BRAHLGAH THE DANCING BIRD

Brälgah Numbardee was very fond of going out hunting with her young daughter Brälgah. Her tribe used to tell her she was foolish to do so. That some day the Wurrawilberoo would catch them.

It was not for old Brälgah Numbardee that the Daens cared, but all the camp were proud of young Brälgah. She was the merriest girl and the best dancer of all her tribe, the women of whom were for the most part content to click the boomerangs, beat their rolled-up opossum-skin rugs, and sing, in voices from shrill to sweet, the corroboree songs, while the men danced; but not so Brälgah. She must dance too, and not only the dances she saw the rest dance, but new ones which she taught herself, for every song she heard she set to steps. Sometimes, with laughing eyes, she would whirl round like a boolee, or whirlwind. Then suddenly she would change to a stately measure. Then for variety's sake perform a series of swift gyrations, as if, indeed, a whirlwind devil had her in his grip.

The fame of her dancing spread abroad, and proud indeed was the tribe to whom she belonged, hence their anxiety for her safety, and their dread that the Wurrawilberoo would catch her.

The Wurrawilberoo were two cannibals who lived in the scrub alone.

But in spite of all warnings Brälgah Numbardee continued to hunt as usual with only her daughter for companion.

One day they went out to camp for two or three days. Nothing hurt them the first night, but the next day the Wurrawilberoo surprised and captured them. They gave Brälgah Numbardee a severe blow. She fell down and feigned death, lest they should strike her again and kill her. The Wurrawilberoo picked her up to carry her off to their camp. They did not wish to hurt young Bräalgah; they meant to keep her to dance for them. They told her so, and gave her their muggil, or stone knife to carry, telling her to fear nothing, and come with them.

She went with them, but when they were not looking she threw the knife away.

As soon as they reached the camp the Wurrawilberoo asked her for it. They wanted to cut up Brälgah Numbardee before cooking her. Brälgah said she put the muggil down where they had rested, some way back, and had forgotten it.

They said: "We will go back and get it. You stay here."

They started. When they were some way off the mother said: "Are they out of sight yet?"

"Not yet. Wait a little while."

Brälgah watched them go right away, then told her mother, who immediately jumped up. Off then went both mother and daughter as fast as they could to their own tribe, whom they told what had happened.

When the Wurrawilberoo came back they were enraged to find not only the daughter but the mother gone, even she whom they had left, as they thought, dead. No feast, no dance for them that night unless they recovered their victims, from whose tracks they found that Brälgah had actually been able to run beside her daughter.

"She only feigned death,' they said, "to deceive us. We will hasten and overtake them before they reach the tribe. Yea, even if they are with the tribe we will snatch them away."

But the Daens were looking out for them, fully armed, seeing which the Wurrawilberoo turned and fled, the Daens after them in quick pursuit, but they failed to overtake them; and, fearing to follow them too far lest a trap lay ready for them, they returned to the camp. But so wroth were they at the attempt to capture their prized Brälgah that a council was held, and the destruction of the Wurrawilberoo determined upon. Two of the cleverest wirreenuns said they would send their Mullee Mullees in whirlwinds after the enemy to catch them.

This they did. Whirling along went the boolees with the Mullee Mullees in them. Quickly they went along the track of the Wurrawilberoo, whom they soon headed, turning them back towards the camp whence they had fled.

"We will go," said one of the Wurrawilberoo to the other, "back to the camp, ahead of these whirlwinds. We will seize the girl and her mother, and fly in another direction. The whirlwinds will miss us in the camp and seize others. We will not be baulked. Young Brälgah shall be ours to dance before us, and her mother shall make our supper to-night."

On, on they fled before the whirlwinds, which gained both size and pace as they followed them.

The Daens were so astonished at seeing the Wurrawilberoo returning straight towards them, the whirlwinds after them, that they never thought of arming themselves. Into the midst of them rushed the Wurrawilberoo. One seized Brälgah the mother, the other young Brälgah, and before the astonished Daens realised their coming they had gone some distance along the edge of the plain.

"Bring your weapons," roared the Mullee Mullees in the whirlwinds to the Daens as they swirled through the camp after the enemy.

The Wurrawilberoo carrying young Brälgah was ahead. The other, finding the whirlwinds were gaining on them, dropped his burden, Brälgah Numbardee, and ran on. Just in front of them were two huge balah trees. Feeling that the whirlwinds, which they now knew must have spirits in them, were already lifting them from their feet, the Wurrawilberoo clung to the balah trees, the one who had captured young Brälgah still holding her with one arm while he grasped the tree with the other.

"Let the girl go," shouted the other to him. "Save yourself."

"They shall never have her," he answered savagely. "If I have to lose her they shall not get her."

Then as the whirlwinds howled round them, tearing up everything in a wild fury, the balah trees now in their grasp creaking and groaning, Wurrawilberoo muttered a sort of incantation and released young Brälgah. As she slipped from his grasp came a shout of joy from the Daens, who were just in the wake of the whirlwinds; they had their spears poised, but had been frightened to throw for fear of injuring Brälgah.

Now that she was free they called aloud: "Gubbah youl gingnee! Gubbah youl gingnee!"

But their joy was short-lived. The whirlwinds wound round the balah trees to which the Wurrawilberoo clung, and dragged them from the roots before the men could leave go. Up, up the whirlwinds carried the trees, the men still clinging to them, until they reached the sky; there they planted them not far from the Milky Way. And there they are still, two dark spots, called Wurrawilberoo, for the two cannibals have lived in them ever since, being dreaded by all who have to pass along the Warrambool, or Milky Way. Where are camped many old Daens, cooking the grubs they have gathered for food, and the smoke of their fires shows the course of the Warrambool. But only can any one reach these fires if the Wurrawilberoo are away, as sometimes happens when they go down to the earth, and, through the medium of boolees, or whirlwinds, pursue their old enemies the Daens.

When the Daens saw their enemies were gone, they turned to get Brälgah; her mother was already with them.

But where was young Brälgah? She had not been seen to move away, yet she was gone. All round the plain they looked. They saw only a tall bird walking across it. They went to the place whence the trees had been wrenched. They scanned the ground for tracks, but saw none of Brälgah going away. Only those of the big crane-like bird now on the plain. Wurrawilberoo must have seized her again and taken her after all, they said.

As soon as the Mullee Mullees, which had animated the whirlwinds, returned from placing the balah trees and the Wurrawilberoo in the sky, the Daens asked them if they had left her there.

No Brälgah they said had gone to the sky. Surely the Daens had seen Wurrawilberoo let her go.

Then where was she?

That no one could say, and none thought of asking the big bird on the plain. All mourned for Brälgah as for one dead. Her spirit, they said, would haunt the camp because they could not find her body to bury it, though they knew she must be dead, otherwise would she not return to them?

They moved their camp away to the other side of the plain.

After a while they noticed that a number of birds, like the one they had seen on the plain at the time of Brälgah's disappearance, came feeding round not far from, their camp, and after feeding for a while these birds would begin to corroboree; such a strange corroboree, of which one bird taller than the others was seemingly a leader.

This corroboree was so human and like no movements of any other birds, like indeed nothing of the sort that the Daens had ever seen, unless it were the dances of the lost Brälgah.

Out on to a clear space the leader would lead her troupe, There would be much craning of necks, and bowing, pirouetting, stately measured changing of places; then gyrating with wings extended, just as Brälgah had been wont to fling her arms, before she madly whirled around and around as these birds did now, seeing which likeness the Daens called: "Brälgah! Brälgah!"

The bird seemed to understand them, for it looked towards them, then led its troupe into wilder, and more intricate, figures of the corroboree.

As time went on the leader of the birds was seen no more, but so well had her troupe learned the corroborees that they went through the same grotesque performances as in her time.

The old Daens died who remembered the dancing girl Brälgah, but all these dancing birds were known for ever by her name.

When Brälgah Numbardee died she was taken to the sky, there to live for ever with her daughter Brälgah, both known to us as the Clouds of Magellan, to the Daens as the Brälgah.

There Brälgah Numbardee learned that the Wurrawilberoo by his incantation had changed her daughter into the dancing bird, which shape she had to keep as long as she lived on earth.

Afterwards, if ever the Daens saw a boolee speeding along near their camp the women would cry, "Wurrawilberoo," clutch their children and bury their heads in their rugs; the men would seize their weapons and hurl them at the ever-feared and hated capturers of Brälgah.

HOW THE SUN WAS MADE

For a long time there was no sun, only a moon and stars. That was before there were men on the earth, only birds and beasts, all of which were many sizes larger than they are now.

One day, Dinewan, the emu, and Brälgah, the native companion, were on a large plain near the Murrumbidgee. There they were quarrelling and fighting. Brälgah, in her rage, rushed to the nest of Dinewan, seized from it one of the huge eggs in it, which she threw with all her force up to the sky. There it broke on a heap of firewood, which burst into a flame as the yellow yolk spilt all over it, which flame lit up the world below, to the astonishment of everything on it. They had only been used to the semi-darkness, and were dazzled by such brightness.

A good spirit who lived in the sky saw how bright and beautiful the earth looked when lit up by this blaze. He thought it would be a good thing to make a fire every day, which from that time he has done. All night he and his attendant spirits collect wood, and heap it up. When the heap is nearly big enough they send out the morning star to warn those on earth that the fire will soon be lit.

They, however, found this warning was not sufficient, for those who slept saw it not. Then they thought they must have some noise made at dawn of day to herald the coming of the sun and waken the sleepers. But they could not decide upon to whom should be given this office for a long time.

At last one evening they heard the laughter of Gougourgahgah, the laughing jackass, ringing through the air. "That is the noise we want," they said. Then they told Gougourgahgah that as the morning star faded and the day dawned he was every morning to laugh his loudest, that his laughter might awaken all sleepers before sunrise. If he would not agree to do this then no more would they light the sun-fire, but let the earth be ever in twilight again.

But Gougourgahgah saved the light for the world, and agreed to laugh his loudest at every dawn of day, which he has done ever since, making the air ring with his loud cackling "gou-gour-gah-gah, gou-gour-gah-gah, gou-gour-gah-gah."

When the spirits first light the fire it does not throw out much heat. But in the middle of the day when the whole heap of firewood is in a blaze, the heat is fierce. After that it begins to die gradually away until only the red coals are left at sunset, and they quickly die out, except a few the spirits cover up with clouds, and save to light the heap of wood they get ready for the next day.

Children are not allowed to imitate the laughter of Gougourgahgah, lest he should hear them and cease his morning cry. If children do laugh as he does, an extra tooth grows above their eye-tooth, so that they carry a mark of their mockery in punishment for it, for well do the good spirits know that if ever a time comes wherein the Gougourgahgahs cease laughing to herald the sun, then the time will have come when no more Daens are seen in the land, and darkness will reign once more.

STURT'S DESERT PEA, THE BLOOD FLOWER

Great was the talking in the camp one morning of the river tribe, for during the night Wimbakobolo had fled, taking with him Purleemil, the promised bride of Tirlta. The elders sat together and planned how to capture them. While they were talking the young men came and told them that the tracks of the fugitives were leading towards the large Boulka, or lake, where was camped a hunting expedition, part of a tribe from the back country, of whom the father of Wimbakobolo had been one.

Then the elders knew the fugitives must be going to take refuge with this tribe. They called the fighting men together, and they said: "Gather ye your weapons, we shall go to this tribe and demand that they give us the fugitives. Wimbakobolo shall we slay, Purleemil shall be Tirlta's to slay or keep as it pleases him."

Soon they went forward, after having painted themselves in full war paint and armed themselves with many weapons. For two days they followed the track. On the third day they saw the camp fires; then they sent their messengers to the tribe, whose elders received them and listened to their request that Wimbakobolo and Purleemil should be given up.

"Do not send me back," cried Purleemil, "to old Tirlta. Two wives has he slain with his waddy; let me not be the third." And she sobbed aloud.

"Cease your crying," said Wimbakobolo. "I give you up to no man, rather would I slay you with my spear. Let Tirlta," he said, turning to the elders, "be a man and fight me. I am ready but he is a coward. Men of my father's tribe, who have given us shelter, who when we were hungry gave us food, remember that in the days that are past my father was one of you, a great warrior who slew your enemies as if they were ants, so powerful was he. Even as he fought for you, so

36

will his son in the days to come, if you give him your aid now. Long have I loved Purleemil, she with the starry eyes, and her heart has been mine ever. Can a maid at the bidding of the greybeards turn her heart to a wife-slayer, leaving the one she loves, turning from one who is young, strong, and straight, to a bowed cripple? Remember my father before you despise the help of his son before you, and his grandsons to come. We shall never go back to the tribe of Tirlta, rather will I spear Purleemil, my heart's beloved, as she stands before you, and mingle my blood with hers."

Wimbakobolo drew himself up and looked so powerful and fierce a warrior as he stood, weapons in hand, before the elders, that they said: "Fools should we be to give up the son of our old leader to our enemies. He shall lead us as did his father before him, and his Purleemil shall be the mother of warriors to follow him, for strong are the clan of Wimbakobolo, men like mountains as their name tells."

Then an elder turned to the messengers saying: "Let Tirlta come alone out on to the plain, there Wimbakobolo will meet him, and there they can fight. If Tirlta will not, then let him go back, a coward, to his country, and stay there. Wimbakobolo remains with us, we shall give him up to none."

Back to their tribe went the messengers, but no Tirlta came to accept the challenge, and back to the big river went he with the others. Wimbakobolo and Purleemil lived in peace, loved of all the tribe they had come to, for he was a mighty hunter, and she a singer of sweet songs.

After a while when the cold winds began to blow round the Boulka, the tribe moved their camp to where, on the far side were more trees for shelter and firewood, for the winter was at hand.

Before the winter had gone a son was born to Wimbakobolo and Purleemil, and seeing what a big baby he was, the tribe laughingly called him "The Little Chief," and brought him offerings of toy boomerangs, throwing sticks and such things until the eyes of his mother shone with pride, and the father already began to make him weapons to be used one day against the enemies of the tribe who had sheltered them.

And Purleemil sang new songs, which she said the spirits taught her, about her little son, whom she said was to live for ever, the most beautiful thing on the plains of the back country.

Purleemil would sing her songs, and her baby would crow and laugh, and the father would say little, but bear so proud a look on his face as he glanced, from his carving of weapons with an opossum's tooth, from time to time at his wife and child, that all would smile to see his happy pride, and their hearts were glad that the elders had not given up Purleemil to be the bride of Tirlta, the wife-slayer.

The winter passed away, and with the coming of the summer all made ready to return to their hunting ground where the fugitives had first come to them.

But Purleemil sang no longer. The spirits she said told her that misfortune was at hand.

"Let us stay in the winter camp," she said to her husband, "where we have been so happy. I fear we shall lose our Little Chief if we go. Let us stay, my husband."

"That cannot be, my wife, or the tribe would call me a coward, and say I feared to meet Tirlta."

"Better be called a coward, which all know you are not, my husband, than lose our Little Chief. Dark would our lives be without him, he is the sun that brightens our days, without him dark as a grave would they be for ever."

"That is true, my wife; now he has been with us so long life would be dreary without him, our Little Chief. But why should we lose him? Did not the spirits say he should live for ever on the plains, then why should you fear for him, my loved one?"

"I cannot tell. Truly the spirits said so, and yet they say now, as their voices come to me on every breeze, that misfortune is at hand."

"But not for the Little Chief, Purleemil. For the tribe, maybe, who sheltered us, then how could we leave them to face it alone? Come with me bravely, mother of the Little Chief, lest your son drink in fear at your breast."

So Purleemil hugged her child to her, and spoke no more of her fear. And as the days passed merrily in the new camp which was the old, the fears were forgotten, and the spirits ceased their warnings.

One night when the tribe were all asleep unwitting of danger, their enemies who had been waiting their chance closed in round them. Closer and closer they came, led by the crafty Tirlta; too great a coward to risk an open fight, he stole like a dingo into the camp at night, meaning to slay by treachery all who had baulked him of his prey Purleemil, she should be slain with the rest, men, women and children, all were to be sacrificed to his hate. He had laid his plans well, waiting until all fear of vengeance was over and all vigilance relaxed.

Closer and closer they crept, making no sound as they came nearer and nearer.

The Little Chief stirred in his sleep; Purleemil crooned him to rest again with the spirit's song telling how he should live on the plains for ever, the brightest, most beautiful thing on them; soon was he soothed and the mother, nestling closer to the ever loved Wimbakobolo, slept again unwitting of danger.

A dog at their feet growled, and Wimbakobolo stirred; again the dog growled, Wimbakobolo rose to his feet, but even as he stood up he was felled to the ground by a deadly blow from Tirlta, and into the camp rushed the enemy, slaying the sleepers as they lay for the most part, though some had time to seize their weapons, but in vain, to defend themselves.

Tirlta, who for days had known the camp of Purleemil, and claimed as his own victim her husband, having killed him, now with a fiendish yell transfixed the body of the Little Chief with a jagged spear.

The tongue of Purleemil, the sweet singer, clove to her mouth as she saw her husband dead beside her, and her child on the spear of her enemy. Then she wrenched the spear from Tirlta, and the end which had passed through the body of her baby she turned and plunged into her own heart, pinning the Little Chief to her, and fell with him dead on to the body of her husband, and the life blood of the three mingled into one stream.

Thus was accomplished the vengeance of Tirlta, which left not one of the tribe, who had given the fugitives shelter, alive. Leaving the bodies to the hawks and crows, Tirlta and his tribe went back to the Callawatta.

The next season they determined to hunt on the hunting grounds of their dead enemies. But when they, reached them they camped some distance away from the scene of the slaughter, lest the spirits of the dead should molest them.

At night they saw strange lights moving on that spot, then they knew that the spirits were indeed abroad.

The next morning they went for water to the Boulka, or lake. How it glistened in the sun! But was it water? They paused and looked. No water was that before them. On they went and then saw that the large lake had been turned to salt. Then the tribe were frightened, and turned back to their own hunting grounds, for no man likes to dare the spirits. Tirlta said he would follow them, but first would he go to where bleached the bones of his enemies, it would give him joy, he said, to see them. With hatred still strong in his heart he went. But surely, he thought, must his eyes be dazzled with the glare from the salt lake before him, for he saw no bones in the place where his enemies had been, only masses of brilliant red flowers spreading all over the scene of the massacre, flowers such as he had never seen before.

As he was gazing with a dazed expression at them, there stretched down from the sky a spear with a barb that caught him in the side and lifted him from his feet. As he hung in mid air he heard a voice, though he saw nothing, say: "Cowardly murderer of children and women, how dare you set foot on the spot made sacred for ever by the blood that you spilt, the blood of the Little Chief, his mother and father, which flowed in one stream and blossomed as you see it now, for no man can kill blood, for more than the life of the flesh is in blood. Their blood shall live for ever, making beautiful with its blazing brightness the bare plains where are the salt lakes, the dried tears of the spirits whose songs Purleemil sang so sweetly, the salt tears which they shed when you and such as you poured out the life blood of their loved tribe. Here shall you sit for ever before your handiwork, the work of a coward."

So saying the spirit transfixed Tirlta to the ground, leaving the spear still through him.

There in the course of ages man and spear turned to stone as an everlasting monument of the spirit's power, and there at Tirlta's feet spread the beautiful red flower, the glory of the Western plains where the salt lakes are—Sturt's Desert Pea we call it, but to the old tribes it was known as the Flower of Blood.

PIGGIEBILLAH THE PORCUPINE

Piggiebillah was getting old and not able to do much hunting for himself. Nor did he care so much for the flesh of emu and kangaroo as he did for the flesh of men.

He used to entice young men to his camp by various devices, and then kill and eat them.

At last the Daens found out what he was doing. They were very angry, and determined to punish him. "We will kill or cripple him," they said, "so that he, giant though he be, shall be powerless against our people." A mob of them went and surrounded his camp.

He was lying asleep, face downwards, as he did not wish his doowee or dream spirit to leave him, as it might have done had he slept on his back, with his mouth exposed.

In his sleep even he seemed to hear a rustling in the leaves, but suspected no evil, saying drowsily to himself: "It is but the Bullah Bullah, or butterflies, fluttering round." Then he slept on while his enemies closed in round him.

Raising their spears, with one accord they threw them at him, until his back was one mass of them sticking up all over it. Then the Daens rushed in, and broke his arms and legs, with their boondees and woggarahs, crippling him indeed. As he made neither sound nor movement, they thought they had killed him, and went back, satisfied with their vengeance, to the camp, meaning to return for their weapons later.

As soon as the Daens were gone, Piggiebillah crawled away on all fours to the underground home of his friend, Murgah Muggui the spider. Down he went in through the trap-door, and there he stayed until his wounds were healed.

He tried to draw out the spears, but was unable to do so; they stayed in his back for ever, and for ever he went on all fours, as his tribe have done ever since. They, too, as he did, get quickly underground if in danger from enemies.

When the Guineeboo or redbreasts, of whose family Piggiebillah's wife had been one, heard what had happened to him, they lifted up their voices and sang the death wail until its melancholy sounds echoed through the bush, as they rose and fell in wave-like cadences. In their grief they cut their heads with muggil or stone knives, and comeboos or tomahawks, until the blood ran down staining their breasts red, and the breasts of the Guineeboo have been red ever since.

GAYARDAREE THE PLATYPUS

A young duck used to swim away by herself in the creek. Her tribe told her that Mulloka, the water devil, would catch her some day if she were so venturesome. But she did not heed them.

One day after having swum down some distance, she landed on a bank where she saw some young green grass. She was feeding about when suddenly out rushed from a hidden place Biggoon, an immense water rat, and seized her.

She struggled and struggled, but all in vain. "I live alone," he said; "I want a wife."

"Let me go," said the duck; "I am not for you; my tribe have a mate for me."

"You stay quietly with me, and I will not hurt you. I am lonely here. If you struggle more, or try to escape, I will knock you on the head, or spear you with this little spear I always carry."

"But my tribe will come and fight you, and perhaps kill me."

"Not they. They will think Mulloka has got you. But even if they do come, let them. I am ready." And again he showed his spear.

The duck stayed. She was frightened to go while the rat watched her. She pretended that she liked her new life, and meant to stay always; while all the time she was thinking how she could escape. She knew her tribe came to look for her, for she heard them, but Biggoon kept her imprisoned in his hole in the side of the creek all day, only letting her out for a swim at night, when he knew her tribe would not come for fear of Mulloka.

She hid her feelings so well that at last Biggoon thought she really was content with him, and gradually he gave up watching her, taking his long day sleep as of old. Then came her chance.

One day, when Biggoon was sound asleep, she slunk out of the burrow, slid into the creek, and swam away up it, as quickly as she could, towards her old camp.

Suddenly she heard a sound behind her; she thought it must be Biggoon, or perhaps the dreaded Mulloka, so, stiff as her wings were, she raised herself on them, and flew the rest of the way, alighting at length very tired amongst her tribe.

They all gabbled round her at once, hardly giving her time to answer them. When they heard where she had been, the old mother ducks warned all the younger ones only to swim up stream in the future, for Biggoon would surely have vowed vengeance against them all now, and they must not risk meeting him.

How that little duck enjoyed her liberty and being with her tribe again! How she splashed as she pleased in the creek in the daytime and flew about at night if she wished! She felt as if she never wanted to sleep again.

It was not long before the laying season came. The ducks all chose their nesting places, some in hollow trees, and some in mirrieh bushes. When the nests were all nicely lined with down feathers, the ducks laid their eggs. Then they sat patiently on them, until at last the little fluffy, downy ducks came out. Then in a little time the ducks in the trees took the ducklings on their backs and in their bills, and flew into the water with them, one at a time. Those in the mirrieh-bushes waddled out with their young ones after them.

In due course the duck who had been imprisoned by Biggoon hatched out her young, too. Her friends came swimming round the mirrieh-bush she was in, and said: "Come along. Bring out your young ones, too. Teach them to love the water as we do."

Out she came, only two children after her. And what were they? Such a quacking gabble her friends set up, shrieking: "What are those?"

"My children," she said proudly. She would not show that she, too, was puzzled at her children being quite different from those of her tribe. Instead of down feathers they had a soft fur. Instead of two feet they had four. Their bills were those of ducks, and their feet were webbed, and on the hind ones were just showing the points of a spear, like Biggoon always carried to be in readiness for his enemies.

"Take them away," cried the ducks, flapping their wings and making a great splash. "Take them away. They are more like Biggoon than us. Look at their hind feet; the tip of his spear is sticking from them already. Take them away, or we shall kill them before they grow big and kill us. They do not belong to our tribe. Take them away. They have no right here."

And such a row they made that the poor little mother duck went off with her two little despised children, of whom she had been so proud, despite their peculiarities. She did not know where to go. If she went down the creek, Biggoon might catch her again, and make her live in the burrow, or kill her children because they had webbed feet, a duck's bill, and had been hatched out of eggs. He would say they did not belong to his tribe. No one would own them. There would never be any one but herself to care for them; the sooner she took them right away the better.

So thinking, away up stream she went until she reached the mountains. There she could hide from all who knew her, and bring up her children. On, on she went, until the creek grew narrow and scrubby on its banks, so changed from the broad streams which used to placidly flow between large unbroken plains, that she scarcely knew it. She lived there for a little while, then pined away and died, for even her children as they grew saw how different they were from her, and kept away by themselves, until she felt too lonely and miserable to live, too unhappy to find food. Thus pining she soon died away on the mountains, far from her old noorumbah, or hereditary hunting-ground.

The children lived on and throve, laid eggs and hatched out more children just like themselves, until at last, pair by pair, they so increased that all the mountain creeks had before long some of them. And there they still live, the Gayardaree, or platypus, quite a tribe apart—for when did ever a rat lay eggs? Or a duck have four feet?

HOW MUNGGHEE, OR MUSSELS, WERE BROUGHT TO THE CREEKS

One day in the far past a Mungghee wurraywurraymul, or sea-gull, was flying over the Western plains carrying a mussel. Wahn the crow saw her, and wondering what she carried, pursued her. In her fear at being overtaken she dropped the mussel.

Seeing it drop, Wahn stopped his pursuit and swooped down to see what this strange thing was. Standing beside it, with his head on one side, he peered at it. Then he gave it a peck. He rather liked the taste of it; he pecked again and again, until the fish in one side of the shell was finished. He never noticed that there was a fish in the other side too, so he took up the empty shell, as he thought, and threw it into the creek. There this Mungghee throve and multiplied, all that followed her being as she was, one fish enclosed between two shells, not as the one Mungghee wurraywurraymul had brought, which had two fish, one on each side shell.

Not knowing that he had thrown a Mungghee mother into the creek, Wahn determined to pursue Mungghee wurraywurraymul and get more, or find out whence she had brought the one he had thought so good, that he might get some. Away he flew in the direction she had gone. He overtook her some miles up the creek beside a big waterhole. Before she saw him coming he had swooped down upon her, crying, "Give me some more of that fish in two shells you brought."

"I have no more. Let me go."

"Tell me, then, where you got it, that I may get more for myself."

"They do not belong to your country. They live in one far

away which I passed in my flight from the big salt water here. Let me go." And she struggled to free herself, crying piteously the strange, sad cry of her tribe.

But Wahn, the crow, held her tightly. "If you promise to go straight back to that country and bring some more I will release you. That you must promise, and also that when I have finished those you shall bring more, that I may never be without them again. If you do not promise I will kill you now."

"Let me go, and I will do as you ask. I promise my tribe shall help me to bring Mungghee to your creeks."

"Go, then," said Wahn, "swiftly back, and bring to me here on the banks of the creek the fish that hides itself between two shells." And he let her go, turning her head towards the south.

Away she flew. Days passed, and months, and yet Mungghee wurraywurraymul did not return, and Wahn was angry with himself for not having killed her rather than let her so deceive him.

He went one day to the creek for a drink, and stooping, he saw before him a shell such as he had thrown into the water. Thinking it was the same he took no notice, but going on along the creek he saw another and yet another. He cracked one by holding it in his beak and knocking it against the root of a tree on the bank. Then he ate the fish, and looking round for more he found the mud along the margin of the creek was thick with them. Then not knowing that the mussel shell he had thrown away held a fish, he thought Mungghee wurraywurraymul must have returned unseen by him, disappearing secretly lest he should hurt her.

Later he found that was not so, for one day he saw a flock of her tribe flying over where he was. They alighted a little higher up, where he saw some of them stick the Mungghee they were carrying in the mud just under the water. Having done so, on they flew a little farther to stick others, and so on up the creek. Having finished their work they turned and flew back towards the sea-coast. Wahn noticed that the Mungghee came out of the water, and opening their shells, stretched out between them, and uttered a low, piteous, muffled, mew-like sound. Making their way along the mud, they cried as they went for the Mungghee wurraywurraymul to take them back to their own country. But their cries were unheeded, for far away were the sea-gulls.

At last they reached the Mungghee which had been born in the creek. These being stronger and more numerous than the newcomers, soon altered their habits of life, teaching them to live as they did, only one fish in the two joined-together shells; and so have all mussels been ever since. For though from time to time, on the rare visits of the sea-gulls to the Back Creeks, fresh Mungghee are brought, yet these too soon do as the others.

The Daens cook mussels in the hot ashes of their fires, and eat them with relish, saying, "If it had not been for Wahn we should not have had this good food, for he it was who caused it to be given to us by Mungghee wurraywurraymul, the mussel-bringer."

WURRUNNAH'S TRIP TO THE SEA

When the two Meamei were translated to the sky from Wurrunnah's camp, failing to recover them, he journeyed on alone. He was now a long way from the spot he had started from, which was near Nerangledool. He had passed Yaraänbah, Narine, and had reached Nindeegoolee, where the little sand-ridges are, to where the Earmoonän have gone from Noondoo.

He was camping by some water when he saw a strange creature coming towards him, having the body and head of a dog, feet of a woman, and a short tail. It bounded four or five feet in the air as it came along, making a whirring, whizzing noise with its lips.

"What is this coming to water?" said Wurrunnah to himself. When the creature was close, he said: "It must be Earmoonän, one of the pups of the dog Byamee left at Noondoo that I have heard of."

He called out to it, "Where is your old master?" for he thought he would find out if the strange creature knew where Byamee was. For answer the Earmoonän made the spluttering, whizzing noise with his lips Wurrunnah had already heard.

Wurrunnah said: "Has he gone right away from you?" Again came only the spluttering, whizzing noise, a sort of pursing of the lips together, and blowing out a sound like "Phur-r, phur-r."

"Is it true that he has gone for ever?"

"Phur-r, phur-r," came again the answer.

Wurrunnah stood up and motioned Earmoonän back, saying: "You go away now. That will do. I want you there no more. You tell me nothing of Byamee."

At the sound of the name "Byamee," Earmoonän jumped away, saying as he went: "Phur-r, phur-r."

He quickly disappeared, going back to the sand-ridges under which Wurrunnah had heard he and the rest of the strange litter lived, in huge caves, where they imprisoned any travellers they could round up into them. Nothing frightened them but mention of the name of Byamee.

Wurrunnah did not mean to risk another encounter, so he hurried on to Dungerh. On, on he travelled for many days, until at last he reached Doogoonberh, which is on the sea. Seeing a wide expanse of water before him and feeling thirsty, he took his little binguie down to dip some out and drink.

"Kuh!" he said as he swallowed a mouthful before he realised the strange taste. "Kuh! Budta! Budta! Salt! Salt!" said he, as he spat out what he could.

He thought it must be the white froth that was salt, so he cleared this off with his hand, dipped the binguie in again, and again tasted. "Kuh! Kuh! Budta! Budta! I am thirsty. I must go back to the water-holes I passed and get a drink there."

Before going, he looked as far as his eye could reach across the sea. He said: "What sort of flood water is this that has a tree in it nowhere, not even a mirrieh-bush, and is salt, salt to taste? It does not look like flood water at all. It looks like Goonagulla, the sky, with white clouds on it. Yet when the clouds move the sky is still; all this moves and is water, though surely man never tasted such before."

Wonderingly, back he went to the water-holes and quenched his thirst. Then he killed two opossums, and skinned them to make water-bags, or gulleemeah.

That night as he camped out of sight of, and some distance away from, the sea he heard its booming noise, for the wind had risen. What the noise was he did not know.

The next morning he went to see the strange water again, thinking he might now make out a bank on the far side. Seeing a high tree a few hundred yards from the beach, he climbed up it and looked again seawards, scanning the distant horizon for trees or land. He saw only water, a dark troubled-looking water that day.

"There is a thunderstorm in it. This must be the camp of Dooloomai the Thunder, and the roaring winds," he said as he listened to the angry booming, "That is what I heard last night." Then, as he saw the tide rising and the waves chasing each other on to the beach, where they dashed with an angry roar, going back only to come rushing in again higher next time, he said: "There must be Wundah—devils— in it, and they are trying to get me. I will go up that high mountain; there shall I see better." But in vain he climbed the mountain; he saw only the strange water, as far as he could see, water, only water.

Down the mountain he went again, back to the waterholes, where were hanging the opossum skins to dry. These he quickly made into water-bags. He waited until he saw the strange water still as when he first saw it, then he went to it and filled the bags with it. He then picked up a few shells to take away with him. He meant to go straight back to his tribe and tell them what he had seen, taking with him the bags of water that they might taste it and know his story was true.

On his return journey he met a very old Daen. Wurrunnah thought he might know something of this strange water, and its booming voices. The old wirreenun listened to all Wurrunnah told him. He tasted the water, spat it out again, sat silent for some time, then he said: "Surely have then my father's fathers spoken truly when they told their children, that there was beyond the mountains more water than the eye of man could stretch across, water covering a bigger plain than the eye of man has ever seen, water which is full of dangers for man, whom it pursues to its very banks, where it rages when it cannot catch him for the many monsters which live in it, and are bigger, they said, and deadlier than Kurreahs. Saw you any such?"

"Nothing," said Wurrunnah, "did I see but water, budta water everywhere. But the voices of these monsters was the noise I heard, bidding the water draw me to them, and howling in rage when I got free away. I shall go swiftly to my tribe, and tell them what I have seen and heard."

Before going he gave the old wirreenun some of the salt water that his tribe might taste it. He also gave him a shell, one of those he had picked up on the beach.

These shells were afterwards the cause of many fights, one tribe trying to get them from the other. The oldest wirreenun of the tribe always wore one of them at the great corroborees. After many generations had passed away, one wirreenun, in whose possession it was, put it for safety in his Minggah, or spirit tree. And to this day there are fights about it, for he died leaving it there. Some tribes try to steal it, but others fight to protect it.

Every now and then on his road home Wurrunnah had to stay and make fresh bags to carry the salt water in, as the old ones started to leak, but at length he reached Nerangledool again, with enough for the elders of his tribe to taste.

None of them knew where he had been, nor could they imagine what this water was which stretched farther than all their hunting grounds. Any stranger that came to the camp was brought to Wurrunnah that he might hear from him what had turned him back on his journey. But Wurrunnah did not live long to tell his story; what he had seen became a tradition in his tribe.

He had broken the law of Byamee by leaving his own hunting ground, so was not allowed to live long after his return.

But yet so famous was he from his far journeyings that when he died, followed by a terrific crash, a huge meteor shot across the sky, thereby telling the tribes for miles round that a great spirit had passed from the earth. From generation to generation was told the story of Wurrunnah's journey and the strange water he had seen, and at the big corroborees were seen the shells he had brought.

At length the Wundah or white devils came to live in the country, and the truth of the old tradition was proved by some black boys who went down from Gundablouie with cattle to Mulubinba.

There they saw the widely stretching water, with the white clouds on it. There they heard its booming roar. They were terrified, but one boy, more venturesome than the others, said:

"Let us taste it. If it is salt, then in truth this is like the water the old men tell us Wurrunnah saw." They tasted it. It was salt.

"It is true," they said, "that which they told us. We will tell them that we too have seen it, and have tasted it. And we will take back some of these wa-ah to wear at the corroborees." So back to the tribes they took the shells to prove their story.

One of those boys, the first who tasted the salt water, is an old man now. He it is who told me the story of Wurrunnah's trip to the sea.

WALLOOBAHL THE BARK LIZARD

Every day, while the little camp children were playing and their parents were away hunting, a strange little boy used to come to the camp. He was only a little boy about six or seven years old.

Every afternoon, after having played for some time with the other children, he would run away from them, go round the different dardurrs, and steal food out of them all, taking, anything eatable he could find.

When the children saw him thus helping himself, they called out: "Don't touch our mother's things!"

He did not heed them, but took what he wanted. The children used to try and get what he took back. But when they came near to him he shot up suddenly taller and taller, far out of their reach. Having thus startled them into leaving him alone, he would escape to his own camp, the whereabouts of which no one knew. At last the parents began to notice how much of their food was taken during their absence, and they said angrily to their children, "You eat all our food."

"No," they said, "we do not. It is a little boy who comes while you are away. He comes along that track in the scrub."

The parents said: "To-morrow we will wait for him, and see if you are telling the truth, for it would be a strange little boy who could steal all the food we miss every day." Accordingly the next day the parents hid themselves in their humpies, instead of going out as usual.

The children played about, watching for the little boy; when they saw him coming one of them ran and told the parents.

Walloobahl, after playing for a little while as usual, went to the first humpie and sat down, looking round for what he might take. After he had rested a few minutes he helped himself to some food, and was then moving on to the next humpie. But before he had time to go many steps, out the men and women rushed, yelling at him and brandishing boomerangs and boondees, which they soon threw at him. But to their surprise, even as their children had said, up he shot, growing taller and taller, while their weapons fell harmlessly around him. Seizing more they threw another shower at him, aiming higher up, but he grew taller and taller, still unhurt. Then dropping their remaining boomerangs and boondees, they caught hold of their spears and threw these with deadly force at him. As the spears pierced him, Walloobahl fell dead.

As they saw him lying there, the Daens said: "He was our enemy, stealing our food. No need to bury him. We will only cover him with bark and change our camp."

This they did, and long afterwards they saw creep from under the bark a little lizard. And they called it Walloobahl, because they said it must be the spirit of the boy they had killed. And ever since then the little bark lizard has been called Walloobahl.

GOOLAYYAHLEE THE PELICAN

At one time the Daens had no fishing nets, nor then had they the stone fisheries which Byamee afterwards made for them, the best model of which is still to be seen at Brewarrina.

In order to catch fish in those days they used to make a wall of poligonum and grass mixed together, across the creek; then go above it and drive the fish down to it, catching them with their hands against the break or wall. Or they would put these breaks across a mubboon or small tributary of the main creek, as a flood was going down, and, as the water ran out of the mubboon, fish would be caught in numbers in the break.

Goolayyahlee the pelican, a great wirreenun, was the first seen with a net. But where he had obtained it from, or where he kept it, no one knew for a long while. When he wanted to fish he used to tell his children to go and get sticks for the ends of the net, that they might go fishing.

"But where is the net?"

"It will be here when you come back. You do what I tell you. Get the sticks."

Frightened to ask more the children went to break the sticks which Goolayyahlee said must be of Eurah, a drooping shrub growing on the banks of the creeks, or near swamp oak-scrub. This shrub bore masses of large cream bell-shaped flowers, spotted with brown, beautiful to look at, but sickening to smell: where no dheal grew this shrub was used in place of that sacred tree.

When the children brought back the eurah sticks, there on the ground in front of their father was the big fishing net, ten or twelve feet long, and four or five feet wide. Beside it was a small smoke fire of budta twigs, on to which Goolayyahlee now threw some of the eurah leaves, and when the smoke was thick he held the net in it. Then, taking the net with them, down they all went into the water, where two

57

men with the net—through the ends of which were the eurah sticks—
went down stream to a shallow place, where they stationed themselves
one at each end of the net stretched across the creek between them.
The others went up stream and splashed about to frighten the fish
down to the net, in which some were soon caught.

When they had enough they would come out, make fires and
cook the fish. Every fishing-time the tribe puzzled over the question as
to how and where Goolayyahlee had obtained this valuable net, and as
to where he kept it, for after each fishing-time he took it away and no
one saw it again until they went fishing; his wife and children said he
never took it to his humpie.

One day the children thought that when they were sent for
the eurah sticks, some of them would hide and watch where their
father did get this net from. They saw him, when he thought they were
safely out of sight, begin to twist his neck about and wriggle as if in
great pain. They thought he must be very ill and were just coming
from their hiding place, when all of a sudden he gave a violent wriggle,
contorting himself until his neck seemed to stretch to an immense
length; the children were too frightened at his appearance to move;
they stayed where they were, speechless, huddled together, their eyes
fixed on their father, who gave another convulsive movement and
then, to their amazement, out through his mouth he brought forth the
fishing net.

So that was where he kept it, inside himself. The children
watched him drawing it out, until it all lay in a heap in front of him,
then down he sat beside it, apparently none the worse, to await their
return.

The children who had been hiding ran to meet the others,
whom they told what they had seen. They were so excited at their
discovery that they talked much about it, and soon the secret hiding-
place of the net was a secret no longer, but as yet no one knew how it
was made. At last Goolayyahlee grew tired of having to produce his net
so often, for the fame of this new method of fishing had spread
throughout the country; even strange tribes came to see the wonderful

net. He told the people to do as he had done, and make nets for themselves. Then he told them how to do it. They were to strip off mooroomin, or Noongah bark, take off the hard outside part, then chew the softer part, and work it into twine, with which they could make the nets though he only, he said, swallowed the fibre, and it worked itself up into a net inside him; but that was because he was a great wirreenun; others could not do so.

After that all the tribes made fishing-nets, but only the tribe of Goolayyahlee could work the fibre inside them into nets, which the pelicans do to this day, the Daens say. And the Daens tell you that if you watch the Goolayyahlee or pelicans fishing, you will see that they do not dip their beaks straight down, as do other fish-catching birds; the pelicans put their heads sideways, and then dip their long pouched bills, as if they were going to draw a net. Into these pouches go the fish they catch, and thence down into their nets, which they still carry inside them, though they never bring them out now as in the days of Goolayyahlee, the great fishing wirreenun, who gave all his tribe the deep pouches which hang on to their long yellow bills, to use instead of the net which each carries inside him, though these are very miniature editions of the original Goolayyahlee's net, but yet big enough to let the tribe still bear his name, which means one having a net.

MUNGOONGARLEE THE IGUANA AND OUYOUBOOLOOEY THE BLACK SNAKE

When the animals were first on the earth they were very much bigger than they are now. In those days the bite of a snake was not poisonous, but that of an iguana was. Mungoongarlee, the largest kind of iguana, which even now in its comparatively dwarfed condition measures five feet or so from tongue to tail, was, by reason of his poisonous bite, quite a terror in the land. His favourite food was the flesh of black fellows, whom he used to kill in numbers. Such havoc had he wrought amongst them that at last all the other tribes held a meeting to discuss how best to check this wholesale slaughter. Many things were suggested, but nothing that seemed likely to be effective. The meeting was breaking up; the tribes could think of no plan to save their relations, the Daens. Just as they were dispersing came Ouyouboolooey to the watering-place. He asked what the meeting was about; Dinewan the emu told him, that Mungoongarlee was so merciless towards the Daens or black fellows, living almost entirely on their flesh, that they feared the race would soon be exterminated if something were not done to stop it.

"And," said Bohrah the kangaroo, "though some of us are as big and bigger, as strong and stronger than Mungoongarlee, if we went to fight him he would kill us with the poison he carries in a hidden bag, and we too should die, even as our relations the Daens do. Most of us have relations amongst the Daens, and we do not wish to see them all killed, yet we know not how to stop the slaughter."

"I, too, have relations amongst them, the hippi and comeboo. My relations must be saved," said Ouyouboolooey.

"But how?" said the others. "We are nearly all their relations."

"Mungoongarlee himself is their and my relation," said Moodai the opossum.

"But that does not stop him from slaying them, whether they are our relations the Murrees and Gubbees, or the others, he slays all alike."

"I tell you that I shall save the Daens from Mungoongarlee," said Ouyouboolooey.

"But how?" said the others in chorus.

"That I tell to none. But Yhi the sun shall not go to her rest to-morrow before I shall have got that poison bag from Mungoongarlee."

"Yhi the sun shall not have hidden behind that clump of Yaraan trees before you lie dead from the poison Mungoongarlee carries, if you fight against him."

"Did I talk of fighting? Is there no way to gain your end but by fighting? Let those who fight die. I shall not fight him, and I shall live. No Mungoongarlee shall kill me."

So saying, away glided Ouyouboolooey through the trees surrounding the water-hole where the tribes had met. When he was gone, the others talked of him and his boasting for awhile, then they all dispersed, having agreed to meet again at the same place, when Yhi the sun was sinking to rest the next evening.

Ouyouboolooey went his way alone, pondering over his plans. Cunning he knew must be his guide to victory; not otherwise could he hope to gain it, for Mungoongarlee was bigger than he was, stronger, quicker of hearing and quicker to move, and above all the hidden bag of poison was his. The only advantage that Ouyouboolooey thought he had was that Mungoongarlee had been invincible so long that he might have grown careless and unsuspicious. Ouyouboolooey decided he would wait until Mungoongarlee was gorged with his favourite food. He would then follow him until he saw him go to sleep after his feast. That would be the next day.

Having thus decided, Ouyouboolooey went near Mungoongarlee's camp, and lay down to sleep there. The next morning he watched Mungoongarlee sally out. He followed him at a distance, saw him surprise three Daens one after the other, and kill them all, then sit down and eat his favourite parts, taking some of the flesh afterwards back to his camp with him. Ouyouboolooey followed him, saw him sit down and eat more, then roll over and go to sleep.

"Now is my chance," thought Ouyouboolooey, as he crept into the camp.

He was just going to raise his boondee to crack the skull of Mungoongarlee, when he thought, "But first I might as well find out where he keeps and how he uses the poison. If I had it I could soon make myself feared of all the tribes as he is."

Thus thinking he sat down to wait until Mungoongarlee awoke. He did not have to wait long. Mungoongarlee slept but restlessly. Feeling something was near he awoke, sat up and looked round. At a little distance away he saw Ouyouboolooey. As he was making a rush at him, Ouyouboolooey called out:

"Take care! If you kill me you will hear nothing of the plot the tribes have planned against you, of which I have come to warn you."

"What plot? What can the tribes do against me? Have I killed numbers of the biggest tribe to be frightened now of the others?"

"If you knew their plot you would have no need to fear them; knowing it not your life is in danger."

"Then tell it to me."

"So I meant to do. But you were going to kill me, though I had not harmed you. Why, then, should I save your life?"

"If you do not tell me I shall surely kill you."

"Then you will be killed yourself, for no one else will warn you."

"Tell me the plot, Ouyouboolooey, and your life is spared, and the lives of your tribe for ever."

"How do I know that you will keep your word? You will promise much, but how do I know that you will fulfil your promise?"

"Ask of me what pleases you, and I will give it to you, to show I mean what I say."

"Then while I tell you the plot that threatens you, give me your hidden poison bag to hold. Then only shall I feel safe. Then only shall I tell you what was planned at the water-hole where the tribes meet to drink; where all said the Daens should be saved and your end assured. And surely it will be so if you do not know their plans."

Mungoongarlee asked Ouyouboolooey to name some other boon, and surely he would grant it; but his hidden poison bag would he give to none.

"That is the way. You ask me to name what I want. I do so. You cannot grant it. So be it. Keep your poison bag. I will keep my plot." And he moved as if to go.

"Stay!" cried Mungoongarlee, who was determined to hear the plot at all risks.

"Then let me hold the poison bag."

Mungoongarlee tried to induce Ouyouboolooey to make other terms, but in vain, so he gave in. Reaching into his mouth he drew the hidden poison bag out; then he tried to frighten Ouyouboolooey from taking it by saying:

"The touch of it will poison one not used to handle it. I will put it beside me while you tell the plot against me."

"You will not do what I ask; I will go." And he turned away.

"Not so; not so!" cried Mungoongarlee. "Here, take it."

Assuming as indifferent an air as he could, Ouyouboolooey took the bag, and went back with it to his old place on the edge of the camp.

"Now quickly tell me the plot," said Mungoongarlee.

"It was this," said Ouyouboolooey, putting the poison bag into his own mouth. Then going on: "It was this. One of the tribes was to get this bag from you, and so take away your power to harm the Daens in the future. I vowed to do so before Yhi the sun went to her rest to-night. Not by strength could I do it. Nor by strength did I try to do it. Cunning I brought with me, and cunning has done it. Back I go now to tell the tribes."

And before Mungoongarlee had time to realise how he had been tricked, Ouyoubaolooey was gone.

After him went Mungoongarlee, but his meal had been heavy; he only caught Ouyoubaolooey up in time to hear him tell the tribes that as he had said so had he done.

"Give us then the poison bag that we may destroy it," they said.

"Not so," said Ouyoubaolooey. "None of you could get it. It is mine alone. I shall keep it."

"Then you shall never live in our camp."

"I shall come as I please to your camps."

"Then we shall slay you. You are not big as is Mungoongarlee."

"But I have the poison bag. Whosoever interferes with me surely shall he die."

And away went Ouyoubaolooey with the poison bag, leaving Mungoongarlee to tell the tribes how he had been tricked.

Ever since then the snakes have been poisonous, and not the iguanas, and there has been a feud between the snakes and the iguanas, who never meet without fighting. But though the snakes have the poison bag, they are powerless to injure the iguanas with it. For Mungoongarlee was a great wirreenun, and he knew of a plant which if eaten after snakebite made the poison powerless to kill or injure. Directly an iguana is bitten by a snake he rushes to this plant, and eating it, is saved from any evil consequences of the bite. This antidote has ever since been the secret of the iguana tribe, left in their possession by the Mungoongarlee who lost his poison bag by the cunning of Ouyoubaolooey the black snake.

WAYAMBEH THE TURTLE AND
WOGGOON THE TURKEY

Wayambeh the turtle was the wife of Gougourgahgah, the laughing jackass. They had a quarrel when the time came for Wayambeh to lay her eggs. She was going as her tribe did to the sand beside the creek, there to make a hole and deposit them; but Gougourgahgah said that was a mad thing to do, a flood might come and wash them away. She should lay the eggs in a hollow tree.

Wayambeh said: "How shall I get into a hollow tree? And even if I did get there how should I get sand up to cover the eggs? And how would the sun shine on the sand to heat it and hatch them out?"

"How was I born, and my mother before me?" asked Gougourgahgah, answering her question with another, going on, "My wife can do surely as our mothers did?"

"I am a Wayambeh, and it is right only for me to do as the Wayambehs do. Does a child not take its name from its mother? My children will be Wayambeh even as I am. I shall go to my own tribe."
Straight went Wayambeh to the creek where her tribe lived. Into the water she went after them. Gougourgahgah followed her to the edge. Then he turned back and sent his servant Wonga the pigeon, and Dumerh the wife of Wonga, after Wayambeh.

Wonga sent Dumerh on to tell Wayambeh to come back.

But Wayambeh said: "No, I will not go back. Let him come himself if he wants me."

Wonga and Dumerh went back and told this to Gougourgahgah, who went as his wife had asked for him. But on the bank of the creek he saw the mother of Wayambeh, so he turned back, for the law of the tribes did not let him speak to his mother-in-law. He sent Wonga to consult her.

"Tell him," said Wayambeh the mother, "my daughter will not go back. He would have her break the laws of her tribe. She shall not leave her people."

Wonga went back to tell Gougourgahgah. Just as he was beginning to do so, out from the grass crept behind him Ouyouboolooey the black snake, an old lover of Wayambeh, who was so enraged at this messenger wanting to bring his old love back to the husband she had left that he meant to kill him. He was in the act of making a spring on to Wonga to throttle him, when Gougourgahgah saw him.

Gougourgahgah made one dart and was on the back of Ouyouboolooey. Clutching hold of him, he flew high in the air, up, up, as far as his flight let him go, then he loosened his hold of Ouyouboolooey and let him drop swiftly, thud to the earth, his back broken. Down after him flew Gougourgahgah. There in his camp he saw his enemy lying dead.

"Twice have you tried to injure me, and twice have you failed," he said; "once when you wanted to marry Wayambeh, who was promised to me, and now when you wanted to kill my faithful servant, sneaking as you did like a coward behind him. But instead of him, you yourself lie dead, powerless for ever to harm me. So shall I kill ever your treacherous tribe, against whom my people shall have a dullaymullaylunnah, or vengeful hatred, for ever. Ah! But it is good to see you my enemy lying there."

And Gougourgahgah laughed long and loud peals of laughter, until the whole creek-side echoed with his startling "Gou—gour—gah —gah. Gou—gour—gah—gah."

Startling indeed was the sound to Wayambeh, for her husband had always looked too solemn to laugh, except when he had to herald the sunrise. She hurried out of the water, and went away along the opposite bank as fast as she could. She thought, as peal after peal of his strange loud laughter reached her, that her husband had gone mad, and if he caught her would kill her. So near the laughter sounded that she fancied he was pursuing her. She did not dare to look round but sped swiftly on. But instead of following her, Gougourgahgah was eating his enemy, and vowing again that so long as his tribe lived so long should they wage war against the tribe of Ouyouboolooey, killing and eating them.

While this feast off her old lover was going on, Wayambeh was putting an immense distance between herself and her old camp. At length she was too tired to go farther. Where she rested was a nice sandy place beside the creek. Here she decided to camp. She made a hole and laid her eggs in it in due course. When the last was laid, and she was carefully covering them up ready for the hatching, she heard a sound on the bank above her. Looking up she saw there a dark-feathered bird, with a red head and neck, peering down at her, who, on seeing her look up, said: "Why do you cover your eggs up?"

"That the sand and sun may hatch them."

"But won't you sit on them yourself?"

"No indeed! Why should I do that? They will be warm where they are, and come out even as I came out, in the right time. If I sat on them I might break them. And who would get me food? I should die and they too."

The red-headed bird, which was Woggoon the brush turkey, went back to where her mate was feeding and told him what she had seen. She said she would like to try that plan, it seemed much easier than having to sit on the eggs week after week.

Her mate told her not to be in a hurry to change her ways; each tribe had its own custom. Then the Wayambeh might be only fooling her. They would wait and see if the eggs came out all right. But even so he would not have her make a nest near the creek where a sudden rise might wash it away. They must stick to their scrub.

At length time proved that what Wayambeh had said was true. The little Wayambeh all came out, and were strong and well. Then the Woggoons decided they would try and hatch their eggs without sitting on them. They could not dig a hole to lay them in, but they scratched up a heap of mixed debris, earth, sand, leaves and sticks. Then the mother Woggoon every second day laid an egg until in the mound were fifteen, all apart from each other, with the thin end downwards. Over these they put some more decayed leaves and rubbish, and outside all a heaped-up covering of more leaves and twigs. When all this was done the parents waited anxiously for the result.

As time went on the mother bird grew restless. What if she had killed all her young just to save herself? She fussed round the big mound which stood some feet high. She put her head in to feel if it were warm; drew it out quickly, delighted to find the nest was absolutely hot. Then, she began to fear it would be too hot. Full of anxiety she scratched away the earth and leaves, thinking the covering was too much. She stopped suddenly and listened. Was that a baby-bird note? She listened again. It was. She called to her mate. He came, and when she told him what she had heard, he scratched away until to their joy out came the finest chicks they had ever seen, quite independent and strong, with feet and wings more advanced than any seen on their chicks before.

Proud of the success of her plan, and anxious to spread the good news, the mother Woggoon ran away from her family to tell all her tribe about them.

The next season the other Woggoons added to the size of the mound, and many of the mothers laid their eggs in one nest, until at last the whole tribe adopted the same plan, thus earning for themselves the name of Mound Builders.

WHERE THE FROST COMES FROM

The Meamei, or Pleiades, once lived on this earth. They were seven sisters remarkable for their beauty. They had long hair to their waists, and their bodies sparkled with icicles. Their father and mother lived among the rocks away on some distant mountain, staying there always, never wandering about as their daughters did. When the sisters used to go hunting, they never joined any other tribes, though many tried from time to time to make friends with them. One large family of boys in particular thought them so beautiful that they wished them to stay with them and be their wives. These boys, the Berai-Berai, used to follow the Meamei about, and watching where they camped, used to leave there offerings for them.

The Berai-Berai had great skill in finding the nests of bees. First they would catch a bee, and stick some white down or a white feather with some gum on its back between its hind legs. Then they would let it go, and follow it to its nest. The honey they found they would put in wirrees and leave at the camps of the Meamei, who ate the honey, but listened not to the wooing.

But one day old Wurrunnah stole two of the girls, capturing them by stratagem. He tried to warm the icicles off them, but only succeeded in putting out his fire.

After a term of forced captivity the two stolen girls were translated to the sky. There they found their five sisters stationed. With them they have since remained; not shining quite so brightly as the other five, having been dulled by the warmth of Wurrunnah's fires.

When the Berai-Berai found that the Meamei had left this earth for ever, they were inconsolable. Maidens of their own tribe were offered to them, but as they could not have the Meamei they would have none. Refusing to be comforted they would not eat, and so pined away and died. The spirits were sorry for them, and pleased with their constancy, so they gave them too a place in the sky, and there they are still. Orion's Sword and Belt we call them, but to the Daens they are still known as Berai-Berai, the boys.

The Daens say the Berai-Berai still hunt the bees by day, and at night dance corroborees which the Meamei sing for them. For though the Meamei stay in their own camp at some distance from the Berai-Berai, they are not too far away for their songs to be heard. The Daens say, too, that the Meamei will shine ever as an example to all women on earth.

At one time of the year, in remembrance that they once lived on earth, the Meamei break off some ice from themselves and throw it down. When, on waking in the morning, the Daens see ice everywhere they say: "The Meamei have not forgotten us. They have thrown some of their ice down. We will show we remember them too."

Then they take a piece of ice, and hold it to the septum of the noses of such children who have not already had theirs pierced. When the septums are numb with the cold they are pierced, and a straw or bone placed through them. "Now," say the Daens, "these children will be able to sing as the Meamei sing."

A relation of the Meamei was looking down at the earth when the two sisters were being translated to the sky. When he saw how the old man from whom they had escaped ran about blustering and ordering them down again, he was so amused at Wurrunnah's discomfiture, and glad at their escape, that he burst out laughing, and has been laughing ever since, being still known as Daendee Ghindamaylännah, the laughing star, to the Daens, to us as Venus.

When thunder is heard in the winter time the Daens say: "There are the Meamei bathing again. That is the noise they make as they jump, doubled up, into the water, when playing Bubahlarmay, for whoever makes the loudest flop wins the game, which is a favourite one with the earth people too." When the noise of the Bubahlarmay of the Meamei is heard the Daens say too, "Soon rain will fall, the Meamei will splash the water down. It will reach us in three days."

BUBBURR THE GIANT BROWN AND YELLOW SNAKE

Bütha the lissome and soft-eyed was promised to Murree, the swift-in-pursuit-of-game, and the time was at hand when he could claim her, for he was now coming back from a Boorah. Back from the tests of courage, back as a brave of his tribe, back with a right to marry. Back to disappointment; back to despair. For first to meet him was Gubbee, the father of Bütha. First to tell him the news of Bütha, his promised one. Told how she had been hunting for honey. How she had come to the nest of a Bubburr, whence she had taken some eggs, bringing them even into the camp. How, just as those who knew of the danger rebuked her for touching these, gliding into their midst had come the mammoth snake Bubburr.

Past them all, straight to Bütha went Bubburr, coiled his form round hers, crushing the life from her. Then swiftly went he as he had come, leaving Bütha, the lissome and soft-eyed, lifeless before them.

"Am I in time for the burial?" said Murree.

"Three times has Yhi slept since we buried her," said Gubbee.

"Then she is even now travelling towards Weebulloo, the heaven of women. I shall be swift to follow her. The dheal twigs are yet green on her path. I shall snatch her yet from Weebulloo."

"Think you," said Gubbee scornfully, "that she who was murdered will follow one who has not avenged her?"

Then Murree paused from slaying himself as he stood, and he said: "There is wisdom in your words, O Gubbee, father of She-who-is-lost. I shall first slay Bubburr, the snake demon." Thus saying, Murree turned to the camp of his tribe.

The days passed, and Bütha was still unavenged. But Murree never forgot her. Nor did he cast one glance on the comeliest of maidens. His heart was with Bütha in Weebulloo. His mind was bent on revenge.

He went hunting with two of his tribe. At length he saw what he wished for ahead of him. A nest of the Bubburrs was there. He did not run straight to attack it, as his mullayerhs expected, but went back with them to the camp.

"Come," he said to his tribe, "come and let us gather the gum of Mubboo."

He told them then why he spoke so, and, seeing his reason was good, they followed him. Having gathered the gum in plenty, they carried it back to their camp.

Next day they went with Murree, and at his bidding broke down the branches of trees some distance from the nest of the Bubburrs. With these branches they made platforms on the boughs of some trees which he showed them. They went on to these platforms, and the noise they made was great; hearing which out came the snakes, the mammoth Bubburrs. Murree and the Daens had been careful that no shadow of theirs should fall on the ground. They knew well that the bite of even their shadows by a Bubburr would kill them.

As the Bubburrs came nearer, and nearer, the Daens made ready pieces of gum, gum of the Mubboo, about the size of a pigeon's egg, to throw at their mouths. Snap went the jaws of the Bubburrs at them. Another pellet ot gum was thrown. Snap! and the jaws, the jaws of death, were closed, held fast by the gum between them. The murderous Bubburrs were mastered. Murree the avenger had conquered.

Seeing the scheme had worked as they wished, the Daens returned to their camp. There they waited patiently, returning in due time to the scene of their gum throwing. They were laden with wood, for they expected to find their enemies dead, and the flesh of Bubburrs was good. Great was the joy of Murree when he saw the gum had stuck their jaws fast, and that the Bubburrs were all dead. His hand was swift to raise his comeboo, and sever their heads from their bodies. Swift, too, were the Daens in lighting fires for cooking the Bubburrs.

Scarce have Bubburrs been in the land since Bütha the lissome and soft-eyed was avenged by the cunning of Murree the swift-to-hunt-game.

Though their name carries terror yet to its hearer. Their size has grown with the time, and fear has stretched their measurements, until even the strongest and wariest feel a tremour when the name of the brown and yellow Bubburr is mentioned.

THE YOUAYAH MAYAMAH, OR STONE FROGS

A family of girls once so offended an old wirreenun that one day, when they were out hunting in the bush, he turned them all into Youayah, or frogs.

When days passed and they did not return, their mother and relations thought that they had been stolen by men of a strange tribe. Rain had come before there was any alarm about their absence, so all tracks were washed out, except the track of the Oodoolay, or round rain-making stone, which had been abroad, as it always was in muddy weather. This stone had the spirits of past rain-makers in it, and could move about, as its tracks proved. Also, when it was making itself a new camp before rain, it could be heard laughing with joy in anticipation of the mud to come. No one was ever seen to touch the Oodoolay, yet its changes of camp were frequent.

Though some days had passed since they were missed the mother of the girls still hoped to find them, thinking they might have seen the rain coming and built themselves a shelter in the bush, remaining there until it was over. She went in the direction they had gone, and called aloud to them. There came an answering call. On she sped to whence it had seemed to come, and called again. Again came an answer from close beside her. She looked round, but saw no one. Again she called. There came an answer from a tussock of grass at her feet. Then she knew she had only heard the cry of Noorahgogo, the orange and blue beetle, which could always answer thus a Noongahburrah in the bush when one of that tribe was alone. She gave up hope of finding her daughters, and being weak and hungry she looked round for food.

Soon she saw some tracks of Youayah, or earth frogs, and finding where they were, she began to dig them out. Fine large Youayah they were, the largest she had ever seen.

"What a feed I shall have," she said aloud.

There came a startlingly melancholy cry from the frogs, who seemed to be gazing fixedly at her. But taking no notice she went on: "I think I shall eat them here. I am very hungry, and if I take them to the camp the others will want some."

She stooped to pick them up, but such a crying came as surely never frogs made before, and so piteously they looked at her that she began to feel there was something strange about these frogs, and she dropped the one she held in her hand.

"But I am stupid," she said, "to take notice of a frog's cry. I would be mad to leave such a good feed here." And again she stooped to pick them up.

Again came their croaking cries intensified. And the cries seemed to frame themselves into the words: "You must not eat us. You are our mother. We are the girls you lost. The old wirreenun changed us into frogs because we but laughed at the mäh of his tribe, saying the back of it, the back of the emu, was humped as was his. You cannot eat us." And loud was the croaking, and so frightened was the woman that she turned and sped quickly through the bush back to the camp with the mournful cry still ringing in her ears, and a vision of the piteous eyes ever before her.

She went straight to the old wirreenun and said: "Did you change my girls into youayah, which are crying now even in the bush?"

"I did so," said he, quite proud the woman had seen proof of his power.

"Why did you so? Why should you leave me to grow old with no daughter to care for me?"

"Did you not choose their father rather than me? Why should I think of you now? Let their father change them again. Surely he is more powerful than I am, since you chose him before me? I am but a humped-back one, so your girls said, even as they said my mäh was, the dinewan. Well you must know that to scoff at the mäh of a man is to make war with his tribe, yet I war not; I but turn your daughters into such as have voices which none heed; no more can they scoff at the back of a dinewan. Go, woman, eat them. Youayah is food that is good." So he taunted the woman who once in her youth had scorned him.

"How should I, a mother, eat her young? What talk is that you make? But alas! surely another will find them and eat them. Only you can save them. Change them again, I pray you, so that none can eat them. Never again shall they scoff at a dinewan. Never again will I scorn you; I will come to your dardurr for ever."

"Why should I take you to my dardurr now you are old, when you came not young?" And he turned away, going on with the carving he was making on a boomerang with an opossum's tooth.

"Change, oh change them, I pray you, so that none can eat them. I will give you the dooree, or grunting dayoorl, of my father's father's fathers to be yours for ever. No one but its rightful owner can use it, for does it not grunt when a stranger touches it? This stone, which of old belonged to the wirreenuns of my father's tribe, I will give you, this stone which alone of all dayoorls has a voice."

"Bring me the dooree," said the wirreenun, "and I promise to change your girls so that they shall never be eaten."

The woman brought the magical stone of her forefathers, her greatest possession, which grunted as she laid it at the wirreenun's feet.

"Now go," said the wirreenun, "into the bush, there you will find your daughters, and find I have kept my promise. Even now they are so that surely no one could eat them."

Back on her tracks went the woman to where she had seen the Youayah. Hopefully she went expecting to see her daughters again. But when she reached the place there were the frogs still.

"Oh, my daughters, my daughters! Shall I never see you more as you once were?" And she wailed aloud as if mourning the dead. But no answer came from the Youayah. Nor did they look towards her.

Wailing, she stooped to pick one up.

"The wirreenun tricked me," she said; "surely indeed no one will ever eat them, for they are turned into stone."

And so it was. Some were of plain grey stone, and some with a stripe of green on them, just as the frogs had been marked. Her daughters would be stone frogs for ever, as were the frogs that Birrahgnooloo and Cunnumbeillee had dug, and left for cooking before they took that fatal plunge into the Spring Cowrigul, whence the Kurreahs took them down the Narrin, and whither Byamee followed them after changing the food they had gathered into stones to mark the spot for ever. And there at the spring were the stone frogs still, as the mother knew, and now she saw their fellow in these the wirreenun had changed, these who had once been her girls but now were Youayah Mayamah.

A LEGEND OF THE FLOWERS

After Byamee left the earth, having gone to dwell in Bullimah, the far-away land of rest, beyond the top of the Oobi Oobi mountain, all the flowers that grew on the wogghees or plains, on the moorillahs or ridges, and all the flowers that grew on the trees withered and died. None grew again in their place. The earth looked bare and desolate with no flowers to brighten it. That there had ever been any became but a tradition, which the old people of the tribes told to the young ones.

As the flowers were gone so were the bees. In vain the women took their wirrees out to fill with honey; they always returned without it. In all the length of the land there were but three trees where the bees still lived and worked, and these the people did not dare to touch, for Byamee had put his mäh or brand on them, claiming them thus as his own for ever.

The children cried for honey, and the mothers murmured because the wirreenuns would not let them touch the trees of Byamee, which were sacred from all for ever.

When the All-seeing Spirit saw that though the tribe hungered for honey, yet did they not touch Byamee's trees he told him of their obedience.

Byamee was pleased, and said he would send them something which, when, as now, the land was perished with a drought, should come on the Bibbil and Goolabah trees, giving a food as sweet to the taste of the children as honey.

Soon were seen white sugary specks on the leaves of the Bibbil, which the Daens called Goonbean, and then came the clear wahlerh, or manna, running down the trees like honey, to pile into lumps which stiffened on the forks of the branches, or sometimes fell to the ground, whence the children gathered and ate it when they could not reach the branches.

The hearts of the people were glad as they ate gratefully the sweet food sent them. But still the wirreenuns greatly longed to see the earth covered again with flowers, as before the going of Byamee. So great grew the longing that they determined to travel after him, and ask that the earth might again be made beautiful. Telling the tribes nothing of where they were going, they sped away to the north-east. On and on they journeyed, until they came to the foot of the great Oobi Oobi mountain, which towered high above them until they lost sight of its top in the sky. Steep and unscalable looked its sides of sheer rock as they walked along its base.

But at length they espied a foothold cut in a rock, another and yet another, and looking upward they saw a pathway of steps cut as far as they could see. Up this ladder of stone they determined to climb.

On they went, and when the first day's climb was ended the top of the mountain still seemed high above them, and even so at the end of the second and third day, for the route was circuitous and long; but on the fourth day they reached the summit. There they saw a stone excavation into which bubbled up a spring of fresh water, from which they drank thirstily, and found it so invigorated them as to make them lose all feeling of weariness, which had previously almost prostrated them. They saw at a little distance from the spring circles of piled up stones. They went into one of these, and almost immediately they heard the sound of a gayandy, the medium through which Wallahgooroonbooan's voice was heard. Wallahgooroonbooan was the spirit messenger of Byamee. He asked the wirreenuns what they wanted there, where the sacred lore of Byamee was told to such as came in search of knowledge. They told him how dreary the earth had looked since Byamee had left it, how the flowers had all died, and never bloomed again. And though Byamee had sent the wahlerh, or manna, to take the place of the long-missed honey, yet they longed to see again the flowers making the earth gay as once it had been.

Then Wallahgooroonbooan ordered some of the attendant spirits of the sacred mountain to lift the wirreenuns into Bullimah, where fadeless flowers never ceased to bloom. Of these the wirreenuns might gather as many as they could hold in their hands. Then the spirits would lift them back into the sacred circle on the summit of Oobi Oobi, whence they must return as quickly as possible to their tribes.

As the voice ceased the wirreenuns were lifted up through an opening in the sky, and set down in a land of beauty, flowers blooming everywhere, in such luxuriance as they had never seen before, massed together in lines of brilliant colouring, looking like hundreds of euloowirrees, rainbows, laid on the grass. So overcome were the wirreenuns that for some moments they could only cry, but the tears were tears of joy.

Remembering what they had come for, they stooped and gathered quickly their hands full of the various blossoms.

The spirits then lifted them down again into the stone circle on the top of Oobi Oobi.

There sounded again the voice of the gayandy, and Wallahgooroonbooan said: "Tell your tribes, when you take them these flowers, that never again shall the earth be bare of them. All through the seasons a few shall be sent by the different winds, but Yarrageh Mayrah shall bring them in plenty, blossoms to every tree and shrub, blossoms to wave midst the grasses on wogghees and moorillahs, thick as the hairs on an opossum's skin. But Yarrageh Mayrah shall not always make them thus thick, but only at times; but the earth shall never again be quite bare of blossoms. When they are few, and the sweet-breathed wind is not blowing to bring first the showers and then the flowers, and the bees can only make scarce enough honey for themselves, then the wahlerh or manna shall again drop from the trees, to take the place of honey until Yarrageh Mayrah once more blows the rain down the mountain and opens the blossoms for the bees; and then there will be honey for all. Now make haste and take this promise, and the fadeless flowers which are the sign of it, to your people."

The voice ceased, then the wirreenuns went back to their tribes; back with the blossoms from Bullimah. Down the stone ladder, which had been cut by the spirits for the coming of Byamee, they went; across the wogghees and over the moorillahs back to the camp of their tribes. Their people flocked round them, gazing with wonder-opened eyes at the blossoms the wirreenuns carried. Fresh as when they left Bullimah were these flowers, filling the air with fragrance. When the tribes had gazed long at the blossoms and heard of the promise made to them by Byamee through his messenger, Wallahgooroonbooan, the wirreenuns scattered the flowers from Bullimah far and wide. Some fell on the tree tops, some on the plains and ridges, and where they fell their kind have grown ever since.

The name of the spot where the wirreenuns first showed the flowers and scattered them; is still called Ghirraween, the place of flowers. There, after the bees of Byamee had made Yarrageh blow the rain down the mountain of Oobi Oobi to soften the frost-hardened ground, green grasses shot up framing fragrant bright flowers of many hues. And the trees and shrubs blossomed thickly again, and the earth was covered with cool grass and flowers as when Byamee walked on it.

It is the work of the bees of Byamee to make Yarrageh the east wind blow the rain down the mountain, that the trees may blossom and the earth bees make honey.

Gladly does Yarrageh do the bidding of the bees, lighting the face of the earth with the smile of rain-water, for are not the Gwaimuthen his relations? The Gwaimuthen whose dark blood is warm as is his. And the messengers who come in the drought, bringing manna, are the black ants, who bring the goonbean on to the leaves, and the little grey birds called Dulloorah, who bring the wahlerh, or liquid manna.

And when they come the Daens say: "A time of drought is here, a great drought on all the land. Few are the flowers anywhere, and the grass-seed has gone. But goonbean and wahlerh will go, and the drought will go, and then the flowers and the bees will come again, for so it has always been since the wirreenuns brought the blossoms from Bullimah."

THE FROG HERALDS OF THE FLOOD

When Byamee ceased to sojourn on this earth, and went back the way he had come from Bullimah, up the circuitous ladder of stone steps, to the summit of Oobi Oobi, only the wirreenuns were allowed to hold intercourse with him, and that only through his messenger, Wallahgooroonbooan.

For Byamee was now fixed to the crystal rock on which he sat in Bullimah, as was also Birrahgnooloo. The tops of their bodies were as they had been on earth, but the lower parts were merged into the crystal rock.

Wallahgooroonbooan, Baillahburrah and Cunnumbeillee alone were allowed to approach them, and pass on their commands to others. Birrahgnooloo was the flood maker. When the creeks were drying up and the wirreenuns wanted a flood to come, they would climb up to the top of Oobi Oobi, and await in one of the stone circles the coming of Wallahgooroonbooan. Hearing what they wanted, he would go and tell Byamee.

Byamee would tell Birrahgnooloo, who, if she were willing to give her aid, would send Cunnumbeillee to the wirreenuns bidding her say to them: "Haste ye to tell the Bungun Bungun tribe to be ready. The ball of blood will be sent rolling soon."

Hearing which, the wirreenuns would go swiftly back down the mountain and across the wogghee below, until they reached the Bungun Bungun, a powerful tribe with arms strong for throwing and voices unwearying.

This tribe would station themselves, at the bidding of the wirreenuns, along the banks on each side of the dry river, from its source downwards for some distance. They made big fires, and put in these fires huge stones to heat. When these stones were heated, the Bungun Bungun placed some before each man, laying them on bark. Then they stood expectant, waiting for the blood ball to reach them. As soon as they saw this blood-red ball of fabulous size roll into the entrance to the river, every man stooped, seized a hot stone, and crying aloud, threw it with all his force against the rolling ball. In such numbers and with such force did they throw these stones that they smashed the ball. Out gushed a stream of blood flowing swiftly down the bed of the river. Louder and louder rose the cries of the Bungun Bungun, who carried stones with them, following the stream as it rushed past. They ran with leaps and bounds along the banks, throwing in stones and crying aloud without ceasing. Gradually the stream of blood, purified by the hot stones, changed into flood water, of which the cries of the Bungun Bungun warned the tribes so that they might move their camps on to the high ground before the water reached them. While the flood water was running the Bungun Bungun never ceased crying aloud. Even to this day, as a flood is coming, are their voices heard, and hearing them the Daens say: "The Bungun Bungun, or flood-frogs, are crying out. Flood water must be coming." Then, "The Bungun Bungun are crying out. Flood water is here."

And if the flood water comes down red and thick, the Daens say that the Bungun Bungun must have let it pass them without purifying it.

EERIN, THE SMALL GREY OWL

Eerin the Daen was a very light sleeper, and when at night an enemy tried to steal into the camp, to spear some one of the tribe or crack a skull with his boondee, there was no chance of his being able to do so if Eerin was there. For no sooner did the enemy get within spear-shot of the camp than Eerin would cry out: "Mil! Mil! Mil!" which was, "Eye, Eye, Eye," meaning his tribe were to look out, there was danger threatening.

And when at length Eerin died, the Daens all grieved much, saying that now indeed their enemies would sneak upon them, and they be unwarned, for none could hear as did Eerin the light sleeper.

They placed the body of Eerin in a bark coffin which they painted all over with red ochre. Before the ochre dried the oldest wirreenun ran his thumb-nail from one end to the other, then across the coffin, leaving thus divisions in the ochre forming a cross. This done they corroboreed round the coffin, singing one of the death chants. Towards evening they lifted up the coffin and carried it to the grave they had dug. The mourners were all painted, and had leaves and feathers in their hair, dheal tree twigs round their wrists, knees, ankles and waists, also through the holes in the cartilage of the noses. They carried bunches of dheal twigs too in their hands.

When they reached the grave they laid some logs in the bottom, which they thickly covered with dheal twigs, on the top of which they put the coffin, as a wail went up from all assembled, the mournful death wail of the tribe which rose and fell in wave-like cadences.

Then an old wirreenun stood up and spoke, telling them that as Eerin was now, so some day they all would be, and it behoved them to keep well the laws of Byamee lest, when their spirits reached Bullimah, they were not allowed to stay nor to wander at will, but were sent to the Eleänbah Wondah, the abode of the wicked.

After this address more twigs were thrown on the coffin, then the things belonging to the dead were placed in the grave, rugs, weapons and food, which would be wanted on the journey to the sacred mountain, Oobi Oobi.

While this was being done the oldest male relative stood in the grave to guard the body from the Wondah until the earth covered it. He stood there while a chant somewhat as follows was sung:

We shall follow the bee to its nest in the goolabah;
We shall follow it to its nest in the bibbil-tree.
Honey too shall we find in the goori-tree,
But Eerin the light sleeper will follow with us no longer.

Then the mourners wailed until the wirreenuns chanted again:

Many were the days when we took our nets to the river;
Many and big were the cod-fish we caught in them,
But Eerin the light sleeper will go no more to the river;
No more will he rub himself with the oil of cod-fish,
Eerin will never eat again of the cod-fish.

Then, as the wirreenuns paused, the wailing was loud again until they began once more the dirge:

We shall spear Bohrah on the moorillas,
And Dinewan shall fall when we throw,
But Eerin will hunt with us no longer,
Never again will Eerin eat of our hunting.
Hunt shall we often, and oft shall we find;
But the widow of Eerin will kindle no fires for his coming.

Loud again was the wailing, then on went the voice of the wirreenun:

"Never again shall the voice of the light sleeper
Cry 'Mil; Mil, Mil,' as an enemy nears us.
Cracked will our skulls be and speared our bodies.
Eerin can warn us no more with his cry,
Only his spirit can come to us ever, an offering let us now pour to
it."

Then with loud wailing, seizing stone knives and comeboos, the mourners cut themselves, letting their blood drop into the grave. Never before was there such a blood offering. Then the earth was thrown quickly into the grave, while some of the mourners corroboreed round it, crooning a dirge.

When the earth was filled in, all stood in a dense smoke that the wirreenuns had made of Budta twigs, which was to keep them free from the unseen spirits known to be hovering round.

When the grave was filled in back to their new camp went the women, for the old one was now gummarl, a place of death, with a marked tree showing it was taboo.

No children, or women with children who could not walk, were allowed to go to the funeral.

After the women left, all the men stood round the grave, the oldest wirreenun at the head, which faced the east. The men bowed their heads as if at a first Boorah, the wirreenun lifted his, and, looking towards where Bullimah was supposed to be, said: "Byamee, let in the spirit of Eerin to Bullimah. Save him, we ask thee, from the Eleänbah wundah, abode of the wicked. Let him into Bullimah, there to roam as he wills, for Eerin was great on earth and faithful ever to your laws. Hear, then, our cry, O Byamee, and let Eerin enter the land of beauty, of plenty, of rest. For Eerin was faithful on earth, faithful to the laws you left us."

Then, standing round the grave, all wailed the goohnai, or death dirge.

Then the men covered the grave with boughs of dheal trees and swept a clear space all round it. By the tracks on that space in the morning they would know of what mäh was he who had caused the death of Eerin. If on it was the track of an iguana then had one of the Beewee clan done it; if the track of an emu, then was a dinewan guilty.

The widow of Eerin had put mud over herself, daubing her head and face with white. She slept beside a smouldering smoke all night.

Three days afterwards the Daens made a fire by the river. They chased the widow and her sisters down to it. The widow caught hold of a smoking bush from the fire, put it under her arm, and jumped into the middle of the water. As the smoking bush was going out she drank a draught of the smoky water. Then she came out and stood in the smoke of the fire. When she was thoroughly enveloped in the smoke she called to those in the camp, and, looking towards her husband's grave, she called again. Those in the camp called to her that his spirit, had answered; she might speak now. She had been obliged to keep silence, except for death wails, since Eerin's death.

Back she went to the camp. A big smoke was made, and the whole camp smoked. Every time a stranger came the widow made a smoke, until the time arrived when the nearest of her husband's kin could claim her for his own.

For some months after the death of Eerin, every time a stranger came to the camp, early the next morning he would sing the goohnai, or dirge; then each man would take part in turn, until all were singing. Then they all moved out of their camps and gradually closed round into a smaller circle, when they would cease singing, sit down, and, rocking their bodies to and fro, they would cry and wail.

When the time of mourning was over an enemy came again to attack them, but they were saved by hearing the old cry of "Mil! Mil! Mil!"

And so it often happened.

THE LEGEND OF NAR-OONG-OWIE, THE SACRED ISLAND

Ngroondoorie, the giver of laws, customs, and a religion to the Southern tribes of aboriginals in South Australia, became to them as a God, and his promise was ever believed, that, if they followed the laws he had given them, after death their spirits should follow his footsteps over the island of Nar-oong-owie, and thence be translated, as he was, to his home in the skies. The tradition was that his departure took place somewhat as follows. His two wives ran away from him. In going after them he crossed what is now called Lake Albert, went on for some distance over the Corrong to the sea, and along the beach past the present Port Victor to Cape Jarvis. When he arrived there he saw the fugitives wading through the water, being when he sighted them about half-way across the channel—which at that time was quite a shallow one—between the mainland and Nar-oong-owie, as Kangaroo Island was then called.

Enraged at his wives for running away from him, Ngroondoorie determined to punish them. He bade the water to rise up and drown them. With a terrific rush the water rose, and the women were carried back towards the mainland. They tried to swim against this tidal wave, but were powerless to do so, and the terror-stricken pair were drowned, and their bodies were turned into rocks which were called Rine-jool-ang, and can be seen to this day, and are known to the white people as the Pages or Two Sisters. After his wives were drowned, Ngroondoorie walked into the water and dived out towards the island. Where he emerged from the water is a black patch three or four yards in width. He went on to the island, and as the day was hot he wished for a shade to rest under. Seeing none, he made spring from the earth a she-oak tree which is said to be the largest in Australia. He lay down in the shade and tried to sleep, but could not, for as every breeze blew he heard the wailing of his drowning wives' voices through the tree-top. Finding he could get no rest, he walked to the end of the island. He threw his spear out into the sea, and immediately a reef of rocks came from the island to where the spear dropped. He then threw away all his other weapons and departed to his home in the skies, where those who have kept the laws he gave the tribes will some day join him. And to this day anyone who tries to sleep under a she-oak tree will hear the wailing that Ngroondoorie, the greatest of all, heard as he lay beneath that giant tree he had made to shade him on Nar-oong-owie, that island which ever afterwards was held as sacred to him and the spirits of the dead by the Southern tribes of South Australia.

GLOSSARY

Bahloo, moon (masculine).
Bargie, grandmother.
Beereeun, a small grey lizard.
Berai Berai, The Boys (Orion's sword and belt).
Bibbil, shiny-leaved box-tree.
Biggoon, water-rat.
Bilber, a large rat.
Bindeah, prickle or thorn.
Bingahwingul, needle-bush, a flowering shrub with roots from which water can be drained.
Binguie, wooden vessel for holding water.
Birrahgnooloo, woman's name (= face like a hatchet-handle)
Bohrah, kangaroo.
Boolee, whirlwind.
Boondee, club-headed weapon.
Boorah, larger borah ring.
Borah or Boorah, sacred tribal initiation rites.
Boulka, leak.
Brälgah, native companion, large crane.
Bubahlarmay, game played by jumping into the water with a splash.
Bubbur, giant brown and yellow snake.
Budta, rosewood-tree.
Budtah, salt.
Bullah Bullah, butterflies.
Bullai bullai, green parrot.
Bullimah, Byamee's camp (native Elysium).
Bullimehdeehmundi, south-east.
Bungun Bunguu, frog.
Bunna, cannibal.
Byamee, big man (Creator, Culture hero).

Comebee, bag.
Comebeegeeboondarnghealdah, grey moth.
Comeboo, tomahawk.
Coolah, tree with water-holding roots
Corroboree, tribal dance

Daen, black fellow.
Daendeeghindamaylännah, Venus the laughing star. Lit., "A laughing man."

Dardurr, shelter made of bark.
Dayoorl, magical speaking stone
Deenyi, iron bark.
Deereeree, Willy wagtail.
Dheal, sacred tree.
Dindee, pointed stick
Dinewan, emu.
Dinjerrah, west
Dooloomai, thunder.
Doongairah, lightning
Doowee, dream-spirit.
Dourandouran, north wind
Dulloorah, small grey birds.
Dullaymullaylunnah, feud, vendetta.
Dumerh, brown pigeon.
Durrie, bread made from grass seed.
Durroon, the night heron.

Eehu, rain.
Eer-dher, mirage.
Euahlayi, language of Narrin blacks.
Euloowirree, rainbow.
Eurah, a drooping shrub.

Gahreemay, camp.
Garahgah, crane.
Gayanday, man's name for voice of borah spirit.
Gayardaree, platypus.
Gheeger Gheeger, the cold west wind.
Gidya, tree of acacia species, which gives forth a sickening smell in damp
weather, or if in bloom.
Girrahween, place of flowers.
Goodoo, codfish.
Goolabah, grey-leaved box-tree.
Goolahyool, water-holding tree.
Goolayahlee, pelican.
Goolmai, death dirge
Goombeelgah, bark canoe.
Goomblegubbon, turkey or bustard of the plains.
Goonagullah, the sky.
Goonbean, specks on the leaves of the bibbil
Gooweera, small stick or bone, possessing magical death-dealing power.
Gougourgahgah, laughing jackass.
Gubbah, good.
Gubbee, man's clan name.

Gubberah, sacred wonder-working stone.
Guineeboo, redbreast.
Gummarl, place where some one has died.
Gundooee, solitary emu.
Gunyahnoo, south-east wind.
Gurburreh, north.

Illahwaylayah, good-bye (said by one going).
Innerah, mistress.

Kumbooran, east.
Kurreah, alligator.

Mäh, totem.
Marmbeyah, white devil who carries a green boondee.
May, wind.
Mayamah, stone.
Mayrah, wind.
Meamei, The Girls, Pleiades.
Mil, eye.
Minggah, spirit-haunted tree.
Mirrieh, poligonum.
Moodai, opossum.
Moogaray, hailstones.
Moorillah, pebbly ridge.
Mubboo, beefwood-tree,
Mubboon, small creek running into larger one.
Muggil, stone knife.
Mullayerh, mate, companion.
Mullee Mullee, dream-spirit (of a wirreenun).
Mulloka, water-spirit.
Mundehwaddah, north-west wind.
Munggheewurraywurraymul, sea-gull.
Mungoonyarlee, iguana (largest kind of).
Murgah Muggui, trap-door spider.
Murroomin, bark.

Noongah, kurragong tree.
Noongahburrah, belonging to the Noongah country.
Noorahgogo, orange and blue beetle.
Nooroonooroobin, south wind.
Noorumbah, hunting-ground.
Numbardee, mother.
Nurroolooan, south.
Nyunnoo, grass humpy.

Oobi Oobi, Byamee's mountain dwelling-place in the other world.
Oodoolay, round rain-making stone.
Oolah, red, prickly lizard.
Oonah, give.
Ouyouboolooey, black snake.

Piggiebillah, spiny Echidna.
Purleemil, woman's name (= starry eyes).

Wa-ah, shell.
Wahlerh, manna running down stems of branches
Wahn, crow.

www.ingramcontent.com/pod-product-compliance
Lightning Source LLC
Chambersburg PA
CBHW031002090426
42737CB00008B/641